Testimonials for Layton Park

"Layton, you saved my life. What you do is truly special."

—Ellen Radysh, CEO of Medwrite Transcription Inc.,
an international medical service provider

"Thanks, Layton. I can now focus better and control my anxiety, resulting in enabling me to help two teams win back-to-back national women's championships."

—Angela O'Heir, softball pitcher,
Kelowna Ladies Slo-Pitch Association

"I have been fortunate to work with the finest trainers and coaches from Istanbul to Ireland. Layton has the kind of credentials, abilities, and experience that ensure the greatest return."

—Kevin Patrick, Vice President,
Business Development, Brian Tracy International

GET OUT
OF YOUR
WAY

About the Author

Layton Park is a certified behavioral analyst and a certified values analyst. His clients include large sales organizations and sports teams, and he founded the Canadian Hypnosis Institute.

GET OUT
OF YOUR
WAY

UNLOCKING THE POWER OF YOUR MIND TO GET WHAT YOU WANT

LAYTON PARK

Llewellyn Publications
Woodbury, Minnesota

First Edition
First Printing, 2007

Book design by Steffani Chambers and Joanna Willis
Cover design by Ellen Dahl
Cover image © 2006 by Digital Stock

Llewellyn is a registered trademark of Llewellyn Worldwide, Ltd.

Library of Congress Cataloging-in-Publication Data
Park, Layton, 1949–
  Get out of your way : unlocking the power of your mind to get what you want /
Layton Park. — 1st ed.
    p. cm.
  ISBN-13: 978-0-7387-1052-5
  ISBN-10: 0-7387-1052-0
    1. Autogenic training. I. Title.

RC499.A8P37 2007
615.8'512—dc22   2006048808

Llewellyn Worldwide does not participate in, endorse, or have any authority or responsibility concerning private business transactions between our authors and the public.
    All mail addressed to the author is forwarded but the publisher cannot, unless specifically instructed by the author, give out an address or phone number.
    Any Internet references contained in this work are current at publication time, but the publisher cannot guarantee that a specific location will continue to be maintained. Please refer to the publisher's website for links to authors' websites and other sources.

Note: The author and publisher of this book are not responsible in any manner whatsoever for any injury that may occur through following the instructions contained herein. It is recommended that before beginning the techniques, you consult with your physician to determine whether you are medically, physically, and mentally fit to undertake this course of practice.

Llewellyn Publications
A Division of Llewellyn Worldwide, Ltd.
2143 Wooddale Drive, Dept. 0-7387-1052-0
Woodbury, MN 55125-2989, U.S.A.
www.llewellyn.com

Printed in the United States of America

Also in the Next Step series

Energy for Life
by Colleen Deatsman

The New World of Self-Healing
by Bente Hansen

Contents

Foreword . . . xi
Preface . . . xiii

Introduction. 1

One   It's Personal 9

Two   It's the Law! 25

Three   How Hypnosis Works. 29

Four   From Whence We Came
        (A Brief History of Hypnosis) 35

Five   What Is Hypnosis?. 43

Six   Did You Hear What You Said? 51

Seven   What's Up, Doc? 55

Eight   Does Your Left Brain Know
        What Your Right Brain Is Doing? 63

Nine   The Sporting Life. 73

Ten   May the Force Be with You. 79

Eleven You Are Only as Sick as You Think You Are 89

Twelve "Trance-Formation" with Hypnosis. 95

Thirteen   The Biggest Obstacle. 99

Fourteen   Refuse to Set Goals 103

Fifteen   Why Goals Must Be Written 109

Sixteen   Why Goals Must Be Positive 115

Seventeen Specific Goals Yield Specific Results. 121

Eighteen   Your Belief System and Your Goals 129

Nineteen   Beliefs Determine Action, and
Action Produces Results 135

Twenty   WARNING: This Book Will Change Your Life! 141

Twenty-One   If Success Were Inside Your Comfort Zone,
You Would Already Be Successful 145

Twenty-Two   Understanding Your Goals and You 151

Twenty-Three   Your Future Looks Great! 163

Twenty-Four   Gaining Clarity 183

Appendix . . . 189

Foreword

Lucky you! This book is your portal to unlimited potential. Each chapter is a treasure of practical gems, exercises, and examples that let you sparkle and shine.

You will particularly enjoy the mental laws that make you a master of your mind, or a "mastermind."

I would like to add one more law to author Layton Park's fine list of truisms, which I would call "Layton's Enrichment Law": To manifest abundance, read this book, do what it suggests, and then sit back, relax, and enjoy yourself.

Shelly Stockwell-Nicholas, PhD
President of the International Hypnosis Federation

Preface

Mike Douglas, a college professor, told me that the best teachers are often the people who most need the material they are teaching. Such is the case with this material. I say that because I first started studying and collecting material about the laws of belief some thirty years ago, in an attempt to overcome some of the challenges I was facing then, both personally and in business. As a result, I have made some huge changes in my life. At first, I did not want to include my own experiences in this book, because I did not want to expose my failures, brag about my victories, or reveal my private life.

There are misconceptions about hypnosis and how it can be used in business. I was convinced it was important to share my stories about using hypnosis in mainstream business and the results experienced. One of my friends suggested that I do as some other writers have and simply not use the word *hypnosis*, instead substituting more palatable terms, such as "visualization techniques." He felt the material might sell better this way in the corporate world. I considered it, but I felt the subject had been skirted enough. People have been deceived about hypnosis for too long, and it is time to bring it into the light and show how it is now being used successfully in the world of business. I trust the stories and information about this powerful tool will assist you in your journey as well.

Like Dr. Jekyll, I experimented on myself, using the information and techniques I had learned. I made a great many mistakes, and not all the results were positive; however, they will give you insight into why I continued the quest. I trust that rather than judge the Mr. Hyde I have become, you will use these experiences of mine as a marker to compare your own challenges and to see if there are parallels that can be of benefit to you. If you see yourself in some of these situations, then you will also see the value of the information.

In the introduction, I explain why the format I use is important to learning the process, and, in addition, explain how the brain and subconscious mind operate. This is followed by a brief history of hypnosis, including an explanation of how hypnosis relates to the way our subconscious mind works and why it is effective in making significant life changes.

Using a mind-mapping process, we first explore which core beliefs are holding you back from achieving all of the things you desire. We then cover how this powerful tool can be used with the enclosed self-hypnosis CD to make the changes you desire.

I urge you to explore these subjects in more detail through some of my other books and recordings, or other sources.

The events, case studies, and examples used are real, but the names have been changed to protect the privacy of the clients.

I look forward to hearing stories about how using this book has increased the number and quality of your successes.

P.S.: A last comment as this book goes to press. Several people who were given proof copies of it reported having more fun and getting more out of the book by doing the workbook in the back together with like-minded friends or Master Mind groups. Why not suggest it to a group of your friends and see how much more powerful it becomes when you have a group to be accountable to? You will also find their added support makes the exercises more effective. Good luck, and let me know about your incredible results.

Introduction

Follow the directions in this book and you cannot help but achieve the results you seek. Read the book first, follow the directions, and fill out the blanks before using the CD. The book is laid out this way for a reason, and you will find the program much more effective if you follow the instructions.

The information in this book has been tested with clients for the past several years, and the results some clients have experienced are truly amazing. This is more than a book—it is a complete process. If you allow yourself to become engaged in the process, you too can expect outstanding results.

Multisensory Learning

The format of the book takes advantage of multisensory learning techniques. Multisensory learning states that we retain:

20 percent of what we read,

30 percent of what we hear,

40 percent of what we see,

50 percent of what we say,

60 percent of what we do, and

90 percent of what we see, hear, say, and do.

Adults who combine seeing, hearing, saying, and doing experience a much higher rate of success when learning any new task. The idea behind hypnosis is similar, in that the more senses that are engaged in the process, the more effective the suggestion will be.

This program is set up to maximize this principle by asking you not only to read the material, but also to become engaged with it by filling in the blanks and listening to the CD.

Much of the material covered will already be familiar to you, and at times I even repeat material, but this repetition brings it to the forefront of your mind. As part of the mind-mapping process, I designed the questions so that you will begin thinking differently about some of the beliefs you have held until now.

What Hypnosis Is

Hypnosis is one of the most intriguing tools available for bringing about significant change in our lives. It is feared by some and misunderstood by the majority, partly because it has been shrouded in mystery for centuries. Most people still have some misconceptions or reservations about using hypnosis. I will begin by reviewing what hypnosis is not, what it is, and how it works, as well as the most common question and answers people have about it.

What hypnosis is not: Hypnosis is not what is shown in the movies. In the movies, someone stares into the hypnotist's eyes or follows his swinging watch and then falls under his spell, doing anything he commands. Later, when awakened, the person cannot remember anything that happened.

All hypnosis is self-hypnosis, and a person can only go voluntarily into a hypnotic state. The client must also have a strong desire to achieve the results being offered to him or her while in the hypnotic state. The stage hypnotist plans his show to create the same illusion as in the movies. What people forget is that it is only the people who want to be onstage who volunteer. They go up knowing they will be asked to do crazy or funny things, yet they still go, because they have a strong desire to be there. Once the volunteers have come onto the stage, about two-thirds will be sent back down to their seats. This is not because they cannot be hypnotized, but rather because the hypnotist is looking for the 10 to 15 percent who will go quickly into a deep state.

For clinical use, a deeper state does not seem to make any difference in the results. In fact, when working with children, waking hypnosis is often used, in which they are not even asked to close their eyes. Onstage, the deeper subjects make for a far better show. The people remaining onstage are first asked to accept simple suggestions, such as feeling that it is too hot or too cold. They are taken though a number of exercises to deepen their state and to give the hypnotist a clue as to who will be the most receptive and entertaining. Of the people remaining, fewer than half of them would do most of the skits, but the audience forgets all of this and only remembers that a few people accepted some outlandish suggestions. The people chosen are left with the belief that they really were under the hypnotist's spell and would have done anything he wanted. The truth is, they voluntarily gave him that power.

After putting on a great show with a very suggestive participant, the participant approached me and asked if she had really been hypnotized. I asked why she questioned it, and she said it was because she remembered everything and felt in control the whole time. She said she remembered thinking that she did not have to respond if she did not want to, so I asked why she had responded. She didn't know—she "just felt like it." If hypnotized people are given suggestions that are within their comfort zone or are for results they desire, they will most often accept these suggestions. Hypnosis is not mind control or amnesia.

What hypnosis is: Although we talk about sleep, hypnosis is not sleep. During hypnosis, the body and conscious mind are in a very relaxed— but natural—state. Hypnosis is now described as concentration on one thing to the exclusion of everything else. The conscious mind is in a very relaxed state and focused on the voice of the hypnotist. While in this state, the body feels as if it is going to sleep, but the subconscious mind remains awake and receptive to suggestion. The only thing that may be asleep is the little gatekeeper who sits on your shoulder and protects your current beliefs by telling you the "truth" when you are given a new suggestion.

How it works: If a new suggestion conflicts with what you currently believe to be true, your small internal voice will quickly remind you why the new suggestion is not true through negative self-talk. For instance, some people may tell you that it is not that hard to quit smoking (or to quit overeating, or to speak in public): all you have to do is make up your mind and do it. However, the little voice begins to immediately correct that statement to bring it into line with your current belief, by saying things such as, "This person doesn't understand" or "They probably never had this problem" or "They don't know how hard it is," or some other negative self-talk. The more you think about not smoking, not cheating on your diet, or any other problem, the stronger the cravings or fears become. While in a hypnotic state, we suspend our critical thinking, and while this gatekeeper is asleep, the new suggestions are more easily accepted by the non-critical-thinking subconscious.

What hypnosis is used for: The power of the subconscious mind is still not completely understood, but we know that the subconscious mind controls most of our beliefs and many of our physical functions. By making changes in the conscious mind, few problems cannot be helped to some degree with hypnosis. Before the use of chemicals, hypnosis was used as an effective anesthesia for serious operations, including the amputation of limbs. Today, it is still effective in pain control and is commonly used during dental procedures and childbirth. It is also highly effective in health issues that begin in or are a result of our thinking, such as high blood pressure, headaches, insomnia, stuttering, and numerous other illnesses. In business, hypnosis is used effectively for a number of issues that may be holding back success, including stress, self-confidence, motivation, improved concentration or improved goal setting, and phobias such as fear of flying, fear of public speaking, stage fright, and nervousness about exams. Hypnosis is also used for removing addictions or habit control, such as weight control, smoking cessation, and stopping nail biting. Look for my other specific programs, offered through the Canadian Hypnosis Institute, to stop smoking, control weight, improve your golf game, and achieve more in your career and personal life.

Frequently Asked Questions

The following are the most common questions I hear, and I trust the answers will help you feel more comfortable with hypnosis.

1. **Is hypnosis a New Age thing?** The earliest described use of hypnosis dates back six thousand years to rites performed in Egyptian sleep temples; however, it is known to have been used long before that time. Many New Age practitioners advocate the use of hypnosis, as do many organized religions, although often by other names. Once you better understand what hypnosis really is, you will recognize its use in many areas of our civilization. Several First Nations family counselors have also taken my training, as they see it as a holistic and traditional approach to healing.

2. **Can anyone be hypnotized?** Anyone with an average or higher intelligence can be hypnotized if he or she is willing and does not resist. You can improve your ability to enter a hypnotic trance with practice. The degree or depth of hypnosis will vary with your ability to visualize and respond. The more creative you are and the more control you have over your mind, the easier it will be.

3. **What if I cannot wake up?** You would be the first, because it has never happened. Every morning, you awaken from the natural state of sleep. While you are not sleeping during hypnosis, you are in a natural state and will feel very relaxed, as though you are daydreaming. However, you will be aware of what is taking place and you will be in control at all times. It takes effort and concentration to get into a hypnotic state. If the hypnotist left you or your CD player broke while you were in a hypnotic state, you would either awake on your own or drift off into normal sleep and wake up as usual.

4. **Will I do or say something that I do not want to?** People in a hypnotic state will not do anything against their moral or ethical standards. If the suggestions begin to exceed the participants' deepest sense of values, they will refuse to participate or will awaken.

5. **Is hypnosis medically approved?** The British Medical Association adopted hypnosis as a viable therapeutic tool in 1958. The American Medical Association and the American Psychiatric Association have since approved it as well.

6. **Is hypnosis dangerous?** There is never any danger to the subjects, although they may be disappointed if they have unrealistic expectations or hold preconceived ideas. Poor suggestions may not get the desired results, but participants will normally disregard suggestions that are outside their moral beliefs.

7. **Are the results permanent?** Some suggestions stay with some people indefinitely, while others need reinforcement. The effects of hypnosis are cumulative; the more they are practiced and reinforced with post-hypnotic suggestions, the more permanent

the results. Self-hypnosis training and tapes are excellent for providing this additional help.

8. **How can hypnosis help me quit smoking?** The subconscious mind controls and drives our habits. The motivation in the subconscious mind must be changed in order to quit smoking. Many people have found that using hypnosis to quit smoking is easy and painless. However, people must really be committed to quitting the habit and want to do it for themselves before hypnosis will be effective.

9. **How does it help with weight control?** Most cases of obesity are the result of overeating combined with insufficient activity, and often the subconscious sees a deep reason or benefit for gaining the weight. As both overeating and insufficient activity are controlled by the subconscious mind, hypnosis is a perfect application for making a change in your thinking.

10. **I am a conventional businessperson. What will my peers think if I use hypnosis in my business?** Today, many professional sports stars use hypnotherapy to improve their mental game. I have also found that many competitive and progressive businesses are now willing to use this tool, including several of the big banks, which are traditionally known for their conservatism. If it works for them, why not you?

one

It's Personal

"Why me?" I could feel my knees getting weak, and my hands were trembling and sweaty. I knew that in a moment my voice would break as I rose to speak. I hated it when the teacher asked me a question, and I hated being in school. I could feel all the eyes in the room burning me and knew that the other students would soon break into laughter either because I did not have the right answer or because of the way I said it. Even after forty years, I can still feel the pain.

I grew up in the same small town as my father and mother had. I graduated high school in a class of nineteen students, eleven of whom started first grade together. The other eight students joined in at various times over the twelve-year period. One of my best friends moved to town when he was in sixth grade, but by local standards, and over forty years later, he is still considered a newcomer.

Our class grew up together: we attended each other's birthday parties, played in the streets, and played organized sports on the same teams. Despite this close relationship, I could not stand in front of the class and answer a question, because I was afraid my friends and peers would laugh at me. I avoided answering questions and would say, "I'm so afraid to stand up and speak because I might forget my own name."

Why would a healthy person feel this way when others in class couldn't wait to jump up and spout out the answers, not seeming to care if they were wrong? What was holding me back? It was only recently that I finally identified a humiliating incident with my first-grade teacher as the key event, now so obvious, that created the self-limiting belief resulting in my not being able to speak in class. I now speak to thousands of people a year, and I don't think any size audience would scare me today. But it was not always that way.

In eighth grade, a friend's father once told my mother that I was in the dumbbell class, whereas his son had been put in with the brighter students. The suggestion reinforced what I thought about myself, and my self-esteem fell even further.

Events during our formative years play a huge role in the creation of our belief system. Our core beliefs cause us to think, act, or behave in a particular way, and our actions are responsible for the results we get in life.

If an event from your childhood still sticks in your mind after forty or fifty years, you can be sure it imprinted a message there. I still recall several instances from my early years that I now know formed many of my core beliefs. Some of these beliefs led to my successes, and others held me back. You may identify with me as you recognize similar events in your own life.

We will explore the effect and power that prejudiced suggestions have, especially on youth. It is true that I did not do well in school, but I would later prove it was not because I was not bright enough, but rather because I *thought* I was not bright.

Other events left me with insecurities, resulting in my having only a few friends. I did not date during my high school years, because I believed I was too unattractive. I was shy, had low confidence, and did not really like myself.

The interesting thing is I now have two sons, Carson and Liam, who are often told they look just like me. Carson's high school photo looks very similar to mine, and when I now look at my sons through the mature eyes of an adult, I see two very good-looking young men who are confident and popular. So what were my beliefs based on? Later in the book, I review this in more detail, including how I discovered the original incidents that formed the basis of those beliefs.

Today, I feel quite comfortable in my own skin and am very confident addressing large groups of people, but in high school, nineteen people were eighteen too many.

When I finished high school, I moved to a large city to attend college. At college, my cousin taught me my first lesson in self-esteem. I was fascinated that he could be so popular and different from me when we shared many of the same physical characteristics and his school marks were similar to mine. I taught him to ride motorcycles and play the guitar, which he skillfully used to spark conversations. When he held court, he was surrounded by young women and many friends, while I could only watch in amazement. I envied him. One day, I shared my lack of confidence with him and asked for his advice. He laughed at first and said that I shouldn't feel that way, as he considered me an equal and actually more talented in some areas than he was. Then, at the wise old age of nineteen, he shared a very important lesson with me: "People will form their opinion of you based on who *you* believe you are."

He went on to explain that people seem to sense what you really think about yourself and will respond to you in a like manner. "If *you* truly believe you are popular or successful, you will be more relaxed in groups and act in a similar manner to popular or successful people. Others will sense your confidence or lack of it, as well as other feelings you have about yourself, and will treat you as you think you are."

At first, I thought that could not be true, as I knew many people who seemed to think they were popular, intelligent, or successful while others only saw them as braggarts. I learned that the language of my own thoughts held the key: "they *seemed* to think," but in fact these people did not believe that to be true. Instead, they were using this behavior to mask their own insecurities, and others could see through it.

I told him I was too honest to misrepresent myself. I disliked braggarts, and I did not want to become one or say something that other people would find out was not true.

My cousin said I still did not understand. "To be popular and liked," he said, "just act confident. Walk into the room like you own it, and listen more than you talk. When you speak, do it with confidence and ask questions about others rather than talk about yourself. Just be cool, and people will like you. The important part is to imagine what will happen in advance. If you can see yourself being successful in your mind, you will find it easier to act as though you already are. Your actions are determined by your thoughts, and your results are a direct result of your actions. So if you think of yourself as a success, you will act as successful people do, and if you act as successful people do, you can't help but be successful."

I consciously used his advice on several occasions when I was in situations where no one knew me, and I was amazed at how effective it was.

I owe a woman named Ellen a great deal of thanks for helping to reinforce these new beliefs. I was playing guitar with my cousin at a party when she arrived and sat down beside us. Every eye in the room was on her, as she had won a beauty pageant for the local professional football team and had also been crowned the queen of the city. I felt I had nothing to lose, and remembering what my cousin had said, I mustered up all my courage and began talking to her between songs. We made eye contact, and I could see she was enjoying our conversation. Occasionally, other young men would approach her, but she would decline offers to dance or join them for a drink and instead chose to sit and talk to me. I didn't get up the nerve to ask her for a phone number or to go out with me—after all, she was the queen, and the doubt was still there—but just spending those few hours talking to her was a huge boost to my ego at the time. One of the interesting things I have learned in my practice since that time is how many other people there are with the same feelings of low self-esteem or the same lack of confidence, and how often they are the very people you believe have everything going for them.

I discovered that we project our own self-feelings outward, thereby getting others to buy into the same beliefs we hold dear. If you truly like yourself, others will like you too. If you don't like yourself, chances are you are not alone.

As I prepared to attend college in the fall, I remember thinking that my fellow students would have no idea who I was, so I planned to put the new lesson to the test. I even recall thinking if this backfired and I embarrassed myself, I could always move to another city to attend college. I was so unhappy with who I was, I felt I had to try something drastic.

If you have ever suffered from self-doubt or negative self-talk, you will know how difficult making a simple decision like this can be, but I was ready for a change. I now know the whole process can be greatly simplified with hypnosis.

I began by telling myself that I was talented, good-looking, popular, and very interested in other people. Almost instantly, things began to change. I had more friends, they invited me to more activities, and I began to have fun. The more this happened, the more I began to like myself and the better the results got. Inside, however, I was still nervous, shy, insecure, and worried that people would find out the truth—that I really was not the person they thought I was. I still had a long way to go to overcome those self-doubts, but I forced myself out of my shell and started the process of changing my thinking and developing more self-esteem. It is actually still difficult to share these feelings with you;

however, I know from my practice that there are millions of people suffering in silence the same way I did. If you are one of these people, you will understand what was motivating me, and I hope my story will give you the confidence to begin making the same journey.

At college, I studied architecture, partially because I am creative and have a love of art, and partially because I could hide behind a drafting board, where I would not have to speak to anyone. After I graduated, I began a career as a building designer. A short time later, the company's sales representative quit, and the owner of the company felt that, as a building designer and sometimes estimator, I would be the best person to be thrown out into the field as the new salesperson. Besides, he explained, without any new buildings to price or draw, if I did not take the offer, I would be out of work in short order.

The thought of going into sales and calling on people, trying to convince them to buy a building from me, was very scary, and had I possessed more confidence, I probably would have quit.

Fortunately, the owner was wise enough to send me to a sales course first, where I learned, interestingly enough, that we are *all* in sales. The program turned out to be a basic self-improvement course concentrating on self-belief, which reinforced what I had learned earlier from my cousin. This new information began to turn on more lights. When I returned to my job, I began implementing and using many of the techniques that I had learned in the course, and I was amazed how well they worked.

I began seeking other courses, and soon I was attending every self-improvement program I could find and reading countless books on the subject.

I learned how to write proper goals and was so enthusiastic that I wrote I would have a million-dollar net worth (which was a lot more money in 1974) and retire before I was thirty. I didn't share this goal with anyone, so I had no well-meaning soul to tell me that the goal was unattainable and that I would be hurt if I set my sights too high. I was too naive to know it was unrealistic, so I set out a plan to make it happen.

Within a year, I became the sales manager of the company. A year later, there was a company shake-up, and at twenty-three, I was promoted to general manager. Before my twenty-fifth birthday, I had quit my job and founded my own company. The courage I needed to do this was all made possible because of the changes that were taking place in my personal belief system. I kept asking myself, "What is the worst thing that can happen?" The answer was always, "I could fail and go broke, but I was broke when I started, so what do I really have to lose?" I became determined to reach my goal and retire by the time I was thirty.

One of the programs I had attended talked about how we use language to express our beliefs and how if we just listen to what people say and how they talk, we can tell a lot about what they believe. The key, then, to being good in sales is not talking but listening. The first building lead I found was a fellow named Ed, who wanted to build a new bus garage for his business using a pre-engineered building system. I got the preliminary information from him regarding size, use, location, and so forth, and then set about creating a design-build presentation. I let my architectural training go on a runaway. He arrived at my office with his accountant, and we launched into the three-ring binder I had assembled to outline my proposal. I explained how I had used the latest and most advanced structural system on the market, which was also the most expensive. I explained why I had used the most deluxe roof and insulation system, as well as the latest in glass curtain walls, accent brick, and a high-tech bus door system. I kept the price for the last page, and when I flipped it over, he almost flipped too.

Ed did some quick mental math to get the per-square-foot costs, then sat up straighter and said rather bluntly, "This is twice what I paid for the building I built last year."

I was taken aback and at a loss for words. I knew I could cut some things out, but I could not get my numbers down to half the price. Before I could open my mouth and insert my foot, the accountant said, "Look, it's five to twelve. Why don't we go for lunch and then come back and go through the numbers in some detail?"

While we ate, I tried to figure out in my mind what I could cut out of the proposal; after all, it was just a bus garage. I thought I could eliminate the brick, reducing the building price about two dollars a square foot, and maybe the glass curtain wall could be replaced with standard windows—that would save at least another two dollars.

My mind was scrambling. Then, suddenly, the accountant said, "Ed, did you decide on a car yet?"

I remembered the lesson about learning to listen to not only what is said but also what is not, and I began to pay attention.

"Yeah," Ed said, "I ordered the Cadillac."

"I thought you had decided on the Olds," the accountant continued.

"I did, but by the time I added in the leather and some of the other deluxe trims, the price was within five thousand dollars of the Cadillac. The Cadillac comes standard with all those extras, and the Olds is still not a Cadillac."

When we got back to the office, I started at the front of the book again. "Ed, when I designed this building, I used the latest structural system, which is the Cadillac of the industry. We could use a standard-shaped building, similar to the one you built last year, and that would cut our costs considerably."

Ed scratched his chin for a moment as he looked at the drawing. Then he said, "No, let's leave that. I kind of like it."

Turning the page, I said, "This roof system I proposed is again the top roof and insulation system in the industry, and we could save some money if we used a standard system rather than the Cadillac."

By now, you can probably guess what happened. I must have used the word "Cadillac" a dozen times as I worked through the book a second time, and Ed decided to keep each option proposed. When we got to the end of the book a second time, I said, "Ed, I know this is just a bus garage, but the building we are proposing is something you will be proud of, as it really is a Cadillac building. We could propose a much cheaper building, but you will have your office for quite a while, and you can't easily trade up if you decide next year you would like something better."

He never noticed how heavily I had leaned on using the word "Cadillac." He just knew that, in his belief system, that is what he deserved, so he bought it. Not only did he buy this one, but I sold him four more buildings over the next five years, and he began to compete with four or five close friends who also bought another seven buildings from me—all Cadillacs.

As soon as I heard his original objection to price and extra options, I was ready to view the problem through my vision of the world, which was, "We've got to get this price down." Had I followed through with that, I'm not sure I would have won that contract. But by being able to see that in his world money wasn't really the issue, I was able to land five years of great business.

What are your clients really saying? Do you understand their beliefs of what the world looks like and how it works, or do you superimpose yours on top and then try to solve their problems with your beliefs?

While working at that company, I continued to attend seminars, read books, and listen to tapes on wealth, prosperity, and self-esteem, and my company doubled in size every year for five years.

By the time I reached thirty, I had over eighty employees and owned one of the leading distributors of pre-engineered building systems in western Canada. My net worth had passed the seven-figure mark. I was even piloting my own aircraft. Several articles appeared in western Canadian business journals about my successes, and I began to believe some of my own press and forgot the basic principles.

What followed taught me the power and importance of using positive programs to change the core beliefs in the subconscious mind.

I did not yet know that success is a journey, not a destination, so I had not prepared myself for a new vision to carry me beyond my goals. I became too busy to remain focused on the principles and lessons that had contributed to my success. I began to think it was my brilliance that had made me successful rather than simple, universal principles. I did not look after my belief system, and self-doubt began to rear its ugly head again.

I had trouble setting larger goals because of a conflict in my beliefs. Growing up in a small working community, I was programmed to believe that people who were rich were generally greedy, untrustworthy, dishonest, evil, unhappy, and not likable. As my wealth increased, I believed I would soon become one of those people. My wife shared the same belief, and she often voiced her concerns about what other people would think of us because we were doing so well.

Part of me was enjoying the success, but part of me felt guilty and was concerned that soon people would see me as one of those nasty rich people. My internal voice began saying, "Who do you think you are, anyway?"

I felt like an impostor and feared that others would soon discover that I was not that smart. I have since found that I was not alone, and I have counseled numerous people who suffer from the same fear. In fact, I now believe it to be one of the underlying reasons that many sports or entertainment celebrities who find fame and fortune suddenly thrust upon them develop so many self-destructive habits. If you have ever felt like you were operating out of your league, in over your head, or getting more than you deserve, you will identify with this feeling. As ridiculous as it seems to your conscious mind, you still can't shake the deeper sentiment. To suggest we self-sabotage on purpose makes no sense, yet how often do we hear of people seeming to do just that? It's not that they consciously decide to shoot themselves in the foot, forget to go to the gym, eat the dessert, or not complete the project, but for some reason they do.

If I had known about the value of coaching or thought of counseling in a more positive light, I may have been encouraged to see things differently and make better choices—but I didn't.

My subconscious mind began encouraging me to invest in riskier ventures, which eventually lost money and reinforced the self-doubt I had in my management abilities. These bad investments lowered my net worth to back under seven figures. I would kick myself at each loss, and the inner voice would say things like, "I knew this would happen." I would go back to work, my net worth would rise, and I would go through the cycle again.

I began to believe that I had become successful because of a series of lucky events and that my good fortune could not last. I worried that one day it would all collapse and that I would become just a poor country boy again. I was sure that eventually everyone would find out the truth.

The mind is a mysterious thing, but there are mental laws that explain how we attract things and events that bring our innermost thoughts and beliefs into reality. I will begin to deal with these laws in the next chapter.

A change in government policy regarding the oil industry brought about sudden and drastic shifts in our business. Rather than search for creative ways to survive the change, it was as though my inner voice rejoiced, saying again, "I told you something like this would happen."

Within two years, the economy spiraled, and I went down with it. I lost my business, my car, my home, and all my investments. My wife packed up the children and moved a thousand miles away, and I was broke and alone. It is difficult to share my failures with you, but I want you to understand how powerful the subconscious mind is. When the positive beliefs that carried me up to the top became negative, they just as quickly carried me down to the bottom.

I told myself I was getting what I deserved in life. I threw a yearlong pity party, but no one else came. I was alone and miserable.

Like many people who lost money during this period, I blamed the government and the economy. I also took it out on my employees, my first wife, and anyone else I could think of.

Later, I discovered a simple formula: $R = E \times E$ (Reality = Events × Emotions). The hardest part of the theory behind this formula is accepting that there are no good or bad events, only events. For example, our city went through a devastating forest fire in which 234 homes were destroyed. As a result, most local people would say that forest fires are negative events. In and of themselves, however, they are not. Fires are how the forest gets rid of old deadfall, creates new life, and rebuilds itself. Our interpretation of the event, or the emotion we associate with it, makes it a positive or negative event. In the case of this fire, the emotions were, understandably, strongly negative—fear, anger, frustration, and anxiety. If you remember early math, you will recall that if you multiply a positive (the event) by a negative (a negative emotion), the result becomes a negative, and so our reality, or the truth surrounding such an event, is that it is a negative experience. Alone, forest fires are neither good nor bad, as they provide a wide range of results. We only consider them to be one or the other once we attach an emotion to them. If that emotion were positive, then our experience with forest fires would be positive.

A year after the fire, many contractors were silently smiling and home décor store owners were happy. Several families that lost homes reported that the new homes they rebuilt with insurance money were much nicer than their previous homes, and they were surprised how many friends and family members came to their rescue with copies of photos and other things they had thought were irreplaceable.

I now attempt to see the positive side to every event and see how I can profit from it. Recently, my wife, Myrna, and I were running with a friend. We came to a rather ragged-looking fellow on a bicycle, pulling a large cart full of bottles. After we passed, our friend shook his head and in a disgusted voice said, "Why don't they do something about those people?"

Myrna said, "I was just wondering how much money he saves us, because city employees won't have to pick up all those bottles or the broken glass they would soon create."

This is the same event, yet seen from two different perspectives.

Another way to change focus is told in a saying Myrna often uses: "Everything will work out in the end, so if it is not working out for you, be happy you're not at the end yet."

With the advantage of hindsight, I now see this period in my early professional life as the best thing that could have happened to me. Over time, the results I received from this event changed from negative to very positive. This will happen to many events in your life as well, if you let it—but too often we spend far too much time concentrating on the negative, and "what we *think* about *comes* about."

This often happens when relationships break down. One person decides it is time to get out and find a new person to share their life with, but every time they meet someone, all they seem to be able to talk about are negative things, such as how bad the last relationship or person was. Then they can't figure out why they can't seem to find a new and positive experience.

I was fortunate, as a short time after that difficult period a friend introduced me to Myrna, a beautiful young woman who had her university degree in the field of family studies. She found it frustrating to be a family counselor, as most of the people she worked with really did not want to change. People are reluctant to move out of their comfort zone, so they keep the negative results they are familiar with rather than risk stepping out to achieve new and exciting positive ones.

Rather than continue experiencing the frustration of trying to help people who wouldn't help themselves, she decided to go into real estate sales. She found she could transfer the principles she learned in family dynamics to sales and management teams. Myrna was soon teaching these same principles to various sales and marketing organizations.

We instantly became good friends and decided to start a new real estate company together. She refused to let negative thinking be part of our conversations, and as partners we spent a considerable amount of time together planning a positive future for the company. We soon saw a positive future in spending all of our time together, so we started dating and eventually married.

In the goal-setting segment later in the book, I will explore how setting the right goals allowed Myrna and me to build profitable companies and a portfolio of real estate holdings, including a twenty-four-suite apartment block and a strip mall, in a very short time.

In ten short years, our accountant told us we had enough money to retire for the rest of our lives. We sold the construction and real estate companies and moved south to a warmer climate.

The accountant was wrong. He either hadn't realized how much money we could spend with more free time or had thought I wouldn't live this long, so I soon decided I needed to go back to work.

This provided us with new insights into life and success. It sounds good to say you retired at forty-six, but being outside of the work force in a new community made it difficult to meet people, and we found the stress of having nothing specific to do greater than the stress of working. As we had both enjoyed our years of training salespeople, we activated our training company, Max-U.com Inc., again and became associated with Brian Tracy International. Both Myrna and I began doing what we love: teaching programs and speaking to various organizations on a full-time basis. One of the first talks we gave was titled "What Will We Do When We Are Done?" It is a program on how to prepare and plan for the day you don't have to go to the office anymore. There are a number of strong reasons why that preparation should begin at least ten years in advance, but the most important lesson is simply that all of our goals have to be seen as an ongoing process, and if we don't project our future beyond the next goal, there is a strong likelihood that we won't have a future. I will also cover more of this later in the book.

Shortly after starting our sales-training business, Ed, the Cadillac man, rolled his motor home into our driveway and announced that he had come to visit for a few days. We were delighted, as he had become my best friend prior to my meeting Myrna, but we had not seen each other for a couple of years.

Ed and I had both seen hard times after the collapse of the oil industry in the early eighties, and we had shared a meager apartment together for a year. Ed was aggressive and ambitious, so it was not a surprise when his new oil-field construction business grew so fast he was netting over seven figures a year within ten years. A competitor made him a buyout offer, allowing him to retire at about the same time I had.

After a year of traveling, Ed also found he needed the activity of working, so he began a large manufacturing company, which employed dozens of people. We were telling him how various programs we offered could help his salespeople improve their performance by changing their expectations and belief systems. Ed laughed and suggested that he would prefer we just hypnotize them. I asked why he would suggest that, and his story surprised me.

Ed said his new business was designing and manufacturing large, specialized equipment for the oil industry. He loved the business but had a hard time selling to new clients. I found that hard to believe, as he had been very successful in other businesses, was a likable character, and was one of the smartest men I knew.

The challenge, he said, was his fear to go to the big city, walk into big offices, and introduce himself to new prospects with big university degrees hanging on the wall. Although he was more successful than most of the clients he would ever meet, he felt intimidated by them. At the time, he thought of himself as a small-town country boy and believed the engineers he had to sell to would not see him as credible because of his limited formal education.

Ed developed his products from his past field experience. They were competitive, well built, and well received in the field. His friendly personality and likable character made keeping customers easy, but he said he had to force himself to make calls to new prospects. He said he would often anxiously circle the block, his hands sweating. He began to miss some appointments because of this inner fear. He did not enjoy this part of the business, but it was the most important part if he wanted to keep growing the company.

A few years before, Ed's wife had quit smoking after seeing a hypnotherapist, so one day it occurred to him that perhaps hypnotherapy could remedy his problem as well. After just a couple of sessions, Ed claimed that his thinking and expectations changed easier and quicker. He said that after the sessions, he looked forward to meeting new prospects and often met with entire engineering design teams and the CEOs of large corporations. He no longer had a problem telling them the advantages of dealing with his company. He said the fear completely disappeared, and the company began growing at an unbelievable rate. Today, Ed has two factories producing his products and is a well-respected leader in his industry and community.

This exchange with Ed sparked my interest in hypnosis, and I began reading all the books I could find on the subject. I found that the principles behind it were the same principles we already used in our programs, only instead of just encouraging participants to control their self-talk with affirmations, in hypnosis the self-talk and belief system could be changed more quickly and easily.

I attended several courses across the country, then became hooked on the subject and traveled abroad to take several additional courses, eventually enrolling in a PhD program. I designed several new corporate and sales courses using the principles I had learned. Many of our more conservative clients were reluctant to try hypnosis at first, because of old myths and beliefs, but once they understood it, they began using it and experienced significant results.

One of my early clients was an owner of several successful businesses who had been asked to speak at the sixtieth birthday party of a good friend. He was well spoken in conversation, but when he spoke in public he had a habit of putting his hand in front of his mouth, which was both distracting and made him harder to hear. We had a hypnosis session, and he gave an engaging talk that evening. He told me that at first it was a little disconcerting, as whenever he felt his hand begin to rise, it would then freeze a few inches off the lectern before he returned it to his notes. He gave the entire talk without once raising his hand to his mouth. When I discussed writing this book with him, he reminded me of the story and said he has not had the problem since.

Our use of hypnosis to assist other clients ranged from correcting other small personal habits similar to the one described above to dealing with more debilitating problems, such as the fear of flying and the fear of success.

The demand for the hypnotherapy services grew, and eventually it became necessary for us to form a new division in the company, which we called the Canadian Hypnosis Institute. Since forming this division, we have been fortunate to help hundreds of people make significant changes in both their careers and personal lives.

The Canadian Hypnosis Institute not only offers services but also is now a recognized school of hypnotherapy that trains counselors and leaders so that they can assist others in attaining the goals they seek.

Hypnosis is simply the art of effectively using powerful mental laws. I was not even aware of these laws on a conscious level, yet they had already played such an important part in my life. In the following chapters, we will explore some of the key laws and how you can use them to your advantage.

two

It's the Law!

One of the world's leading sales trainers, Brian Tracy, often says that before Newton, if an apple let go of the tree, it fell toward the ground despite the fact that no one knew about the law of gravity.

Natural laws cannot be broken; they are consistent and apply in every case. It does not matter if you do not know about these laws, agree with them, or understand them. They act equally on everyone, every time.

Whether you throw something off a building in Seattle or London, it will fall to the ground and gather speed at the same traditional acceleration due to gravity of 9.8 meters per second per second, regardless of whether you know about the law of gravity or not.

The universal laws of mind are the same. They work regardless of whether you know about them or agree with them. I'm sure you have heard of many of these laws, as they are as old as wisdom itself, but now is the time to actually apply them to your life.

I believe the following statement by Emmet Fox to be the foundation of all the mental laws based on the verse "What you think upon grows" (Philippians 4:8):

> What you think upon grows is an Eastern maxim, and it sums up neatly the greatest and most fundamental of all the Laws of Mind. What you think upon grows.
>
> What you think upon grows. Whatever you allow to occupy your mind you magnify in your life. Whether the subject of your thoughts is good or bad, the law works and the condition grows.
>
> The more you think about your indigestion or your rheumatism, the worse it will become. The more you think of yourself as healthy and well, the better will your body will be.
>
> The more you think about lack, bad times, et cetera, the worse will your business will be; and the more you think of prosperity, abundance, and success, the more of these things will you bring into your life.
>
> The more you think about your grievances or the injustices that you have suffered, the more such trials you will continue to receive; and the more you think of the good fortune you have had, the more good fortune will come to you.*

---

* Emmet Fox, *Make Your Life Worthwhile* (New York: Harper & Row, 1946).

All psychological and metaphysical teaching is little more than a commentary upon this basic, fundamental, and all-inclusive Law of Mind.

In psychological and philosophical circles, "what you think upon grows" is a well-accepted phenomenon. So, the key to achieving success in any form is to think only about what you want, and not about what you don't want. Reframe your thoughts to think of health not sickness, wealth not poverty, success not failure, and you will immediately vault ahead of most people.

Brian Tracy gave us similar information in the universal laws of success, a collection of natural laws that affect the way we think and act and the results we achieve, such as the Law of Mental Equivalency.

The Law of Mental Equivalency states that *the world around you is the physical equivalent of the world within you. Your main job in life is to create within your own mind the mental equivalent of the life you want to live.*

Imagine your ideal life, in every respect. If you hold that thought, it will materialize around you.

The hard but vital part is seeing or visualizing the results you want and never thinking about the results you don't want. One way to make this happen is to get rid of the tolerations in your life. If you have chaos and disorder around you at home or in the office, it plays on your mind. If you create order in your environment, you will find order showing up in other places in your life.

It does not matter how you feel about these laws or whether you believe in them or not: they do govern your life. If you are looking for the easiest way to succeed in your journey, learn the laws and use them to your advantage.

I will demonstrate how to decide what you want and then, using these various laws, how to remove the obstacles you have been putting in your own way.

The only thing that prevents most of us from achieving what we desire is our own limiting beliefs. I know you will find the laws in this book of great benefit in taking control over your life, because they have helped so many others before you. These principles are not new; they have been with us since the beginning of time. My goal here is to put them into the simplest form so that they are clear and easy for you to implement.

Read the biographies of any number of successful individuals and you will find they all wrestled with and finally utilized these same principles.

Henry Ford said, "Whether you think you are right or whether you think you are wrong, you are right."

Former President Woodrow Wilson was convinced that the subconscious mind is the gateway to the infinite intelligence of our Creator and can be used effectively. As a result, he developed the habit of writing out clear statements of what he wished to accomplish, just before going to bed. He would read it aloud several times and ask for guidance to fulfill it.

Sir Winston Churchill said, "A pessimist sees the difficulty in every opportunity; an optimist sees the opportunity in every difficulty."

Discover what you really want and how the universal laws will assist you in obtaining it. Learn how to get out of your way by using self-hypnosis to program yourself for continued success.

We will continue in the next chapter by clarifying what hypnosis is and how it will work for you to this end.

three

How Hypnosis Works

The Law of Belief states that *whatever you believe with feeling becomes your reality. You do not believe what you see; you see what you have already chosen to believe.*

Only once you identify the self-limiting beliefs that are holding you back can you remove them.

The subconscious mind holds our core beliefs, and we act in accordance with our beliefs. Our beliefs determine what actions we take, and the actions we take determine our results. For example, we may believe that we are destined to be fat. We may think that our parents and our siblings are fat, so it must be hereditary, and no matter what we do, we will be fat. The action we take because of this belief is probably no action at all. After all, why exercise? It won't help, because you can't fight something hereditary. Even a choice of no action, however, is an action, so the results produced will be to become fatter. Another action might be to keep eating improperly. After all, why diet? You can't fight heredity. And the result is to continue adding weight.

The difficulty most of us face in changing our results is finding an effective way to change our beliefs.

Most programs suggest that the most effective way to change our beliefs is by using affirmations. Affirmations are statements made in the first person and using the present tense to suggest that the desired results have already been achieved. The theory is, if an affirmation is repeated often enough, the subconscious mind, which cannot tell the difference between what is real and what is fantasy, will accept the new statement as true. As stated earlier, if we believe something to be true, we tend to act in accordance with those beliefs, and these actions produce predictable results.

The problem most of us encounter is our gatekeeper. The gatekeeper is the little voice that prevents a new belief from getting through by whispering a negative PS that defeats the affirmation and reinforces the old belief. This PS contains the truth as we currently perceive it to be. Our subconscious believes that it is protecting us by telling us this truth.

For example, someone who wants to become a successful salesperson may have an affirmation that states, "I am a well-paid, successful salesperson." However, immediately following the affirmation, the small voice of self-doubt adds a self-defeating statement in a PS, such as:

- Who do you think you're kidding?
- I peeked into our bank account, and there is nothing in there.
- You lost two deals yesterday.

In seminars, participants often say they cannot give themselves effective affirmations because they feel they are lying to themselves. The truth is only perception. We are all millionaires; it is just that some of us have not received the money yet. You know you can reframe your beliefs; however, many still feel uncomfortable and keep adding a negative PS to each message, thus nullifying the change.

Under hypnosis, we have direct access or communication with the subconscious mind, bypassing our critical thinking and this self-defeating little voice. We know that hypnosis is not sleep, but if anything is asleep, it is the gatekeeper.

As the subconscious mind is not capable of logic or reason, the commands it is given are accepted at face value, and in hypnosis, the negative messages are not added to the affirmations or suggestions.

At times, the information in this book may seem redundant or repetitive, but I formatted the book in this way for a specific reason. It is known that if information is brought to the surface of your mind and repeated often enough, the subconscious mind will begin accepting it as fact even if the conscious mind discounts or ignores the information the first few times it hears it.

A stage hypnotist can give subjects a suggestion they know is not true, such as that one of the chairs onstage weighs a thousand pounds. While the subjects appear to be perfectly awake when they try to move or pick up the chair, they find it impossible to do. If the subconscious mind can believe that a simple stacking chair weighs a thousand pounds, then it is not a stretch that other beliefs can be changed as well. We can all believe, imagine, or pretend that there is a thin person inside of us, that we are successful already and the rewards will soon follow, or that we are confident, cool, collected, and in control already.

People use hypnosis to achieve many goals. Weight loss and stopping smoking are the most well known, but hypnosis is also used successfully to help people overcome a multitude of phobias and other problems.

This answer seems too simple, though. If hypnosis works so well, then why is it not being more widely used? Is hypnosis really the silver bullet? It sure seemed to be for my friend Ed. However, if it were that effective, I wondered, why doesn't everyone use it?

Surely, if these questions bothered me, someone else must have asked them a long time ago as well. If they did, what did they find?

Is it possible that we are all standing on acres of diamonds and no one has noticed? My research continued into the subject.

I discovered that there is no magic to hypnosis and that several of history's major leaders have experimented with it. I became excited as I realized that this largely misunderstood practice may hold the key to entering the next level of success.

I was surprised to learn that there is no mystery to hypnosis: it is not magic, nor is it a secret art passed down by special people. Hypnosis has been with us since the beginning of human civilization, and it is used by a number of mainstream institutions today.

Most people are hesitant to use hypnosis for one of two reasons, both of which you now know are false: they have a fear of having someone control their mind, or they are afraid they won't remember what went on during the session. Relax, hypnosis is not mind control being used by some sinister fellow with a handlebar moustache and a tall black hat, or any of the other things portrayed in the movies. Hypnosis is not one of the black arts, a subculture, or a cult. You remain in control of your own mind, and you will not do anything outside your comfort zone. If it were possible to control someone's mind that easily, we would not have a need for prisons. We could save a fortune just by hypnotizing all the bad people and telling them to go home, obey the law, and not do that anymore. If they were bad, we could tell them to go to their rooms and they wouldn't be able to leave them for a set amount of time.

All hypnosis is self-hypnosis. No one else can put you into a trance; people allow themselves to go into a trance. The hypnotist or hypnotherapist merely leads the client, and the client chooses whether to follow.

Hypnosis is not as mysterious as it appears during stage shows, in which the hypnotist wants to create the illusion that he or she can control the mind of the participants and make them perform things they would not otherwise do.

The truth is that hypnosis is a natural state of mind we all experience daily. Hypnosis can be used for self-improvement as well as in counseling and coaching to help clients make their desired changes.

To understand how hypnosis works, let me first take you back to the beginning and give you a brief history of hypnosis in the chapter that follows. We will then explore what hypnosis is, how exactly it works, and the areas of your life in which you can apply it.

four

From Whence We Came (A Brief History of Hypnosis)

The Law of Growth states that *if you are not growing, you are stagnating. If you are not getting better, you are getting worse.*

Make continuous learning and growth a part of your daily routine.

We forget how much we have grown as a society in just the past couple of generations. Imagine traveling back to a time when people lived in the wilderness and cooked over open fires. I am not talking about taking the motor home and barbecue to the lake for the weekend; I'm speaking of the time way before TV, before electricity, before indoor plumbing. Take a deep breath, relax, and see yourself on a movie screen in your mind's eye . . .

You are living in a hut with a dirt floor. You spend your days hunting various animals to provide you with food and clothes. One morning, you wake up feeling ill. You have no idea why you are sick, and the only explanation anyone has is that you must have taken on some sort of evil spirit. It is easy to believe, because whatever is wrong with you is definitely on the inside of your body, and you feel you must get whatever it is out of you. You know that several people have died after becoming sick, so this could be a matter of life and death. You are stressed but have a strong desire to get well, so you send for help.

Your friends and family gather around you but don't know what to do either. They send for the medicine man (witch doctor, shaman, or faith healer), as he or she has been able to cure some of the people who have been sick in the past. While your family and friends wait, they try to ward off the evil spirit by chanting and beating out a steady rhythm on drums. You lie quietly in the dim light of your hut, sweating, worrying, and believing you will be cured when this medicine man arrives. But where is he? (We ask these same questions today, only the waiting takes place after we drag ourselves into the doctor's office.)

Waiting impatiently, the steady beating of the drums and chanting begins growing stronger and getting faster. You become more and more focused on only one thing. What is it inside of you? Louder, louder, and faster, faster, the beating continues until suddenly, throwing back the flap on the door, the doctor dances in waving a magic stick. The head and face of the mysterious healer is covered with paint, beads, and feathers.

(This was before the use of surgical masks and clipboards, but the effect was the same.)

The healer stares into your eyes the whole time, and you do not want to look away. You do not want to miss any clues as to your cure. Your focus becomes more intense, you breathe more deeply, and you concentrate only on the doctor. As he or she continues to dance, the doctor digs into a small leather pouch. (Today, it is a black leather bag.)

The doctor brings out a pinch of smelly substance, sprinkling and rubbing it on you or asking you to swallow it. (This part is similar to the procedures still used today, but now the substance comes at a much higher price.)

Then, as quickly as he came, he leaves. You fall back onto your bed, close your eyes, and relax, as you are so relieved that he came in time. You are confident that everything will be fine and that soon you will be well again.

At sunrise, you awaken feeling much better. The reason is obvious: the doctor removed the evil spirit.

During this hypnotic environment, the suggestion given is that you will get better. You believe the suggestion will work because you know it has worked in the past for you or someone you know. You have seen others get better, just as your family has now seen you get better. You believe that the doctor really does have the power to make you well, and because you believe it, in many cases, it becomes so.

Fast-forward to the sophistication of modern science, with its knowledge of microorganisms, viruses, germs, and countless other causes of illnesses. We know that the doctor does not have the power; we understand that the power is really in the medicine and that if we take it, we will get better. After all, this message is drummed into us while we watch TV in a semihypnotic state.

I do not discount the value or progress medicine has made. However, it is interesting that when the effect of a new medicine is studied, the researchers must take into account the placebo effect. To approve a new medicine, two groups are prescribed what they believe to be the new medicine. One group actually receives the medicine while the other, the control group, gets a sugar pill, and the results are compared to see what the effect is.

The researchers expect at least 25 percent, and as high as 75 percent, of the patients who do not receive the medicine will experience the same results as those who did. It is not that the medicine is not effective; in fact, the tests often show it is. It's that in a large percentage of cases, just believing the medicine is effective will be enough to trigger the body's immune system and cause it to attack the problem. Just as the patient of the medicine man became better, people can still recover from illness simply because they subconsciously believe they will.

Medicine now claims that a large number of illnesses are psychosomatic in origin, so it is not surprising that the subconscious mind has the power to treat many of our ailments.

The medicine men, witch doctors, and shamans of days past assisted their patients in entering a hypnotic trance and then gave them a suggestion to trigger their body's own healing powers. Archaeologists have found records showing the use of hypnosis in the sleep temples of ancient India and Egypt. Hypnosis is used frequently in prayer or chanting during faith-healing or religious ceremonies.

Science does not completely understand the power the subconscious mind has over the physical health of the body, but it does recognize that such power exists and is most effective when used in the form of a hypnotic suggestion.

The use of hypnosis continued in many Eastern cultures during the Middle Ages, but it almost disappeared when introduced to Western civilization. Today it is still used by some doctors and dentists for controlling pain as well as curing a number of illnesses.

When I first began my practice, the mother of a friend called to say I was playing with witchcraft and should be careful. In the meantime, she was praying for me.

However, I checked with several members of the clergy, and they told me that hypnosis is a God-given gift and that, like an ax, it may be used to serve us or it can be used as a weapon. It is not the ax that is evil, it is how it is used. The same holds true for hypnosis. Most people who know anything about hypnosis at all will agree that it is not in contradiction with any modern religious beliefs but rather has been acknowledged by many spiritual leaders.

I am not a student of the Bible, but it is filled with many stories of various leaders entering trance states. The uneducated fear or condemn hypnosis as the work of the devil because they think it can be used to control others, yet history clearly shows the major churches themselves have used hypnotic suggestion and techniques on a regular basis. At one time, many Christian organizations controlled their parishioners through fear and guilt, so they strongly discouraged anything empowering the individual, including the use of a hypnotic trance. In some areas, hypnosis was branded as witchcraft, and as witches were burned, the practice went underground—even though many of the churches used the hypnotic effect themselves during their own rites.

With hypnosis, we can enter into a deeper connection with our subconscious mind and find a stronger connection to our spirituality or ability to pray.

"For God hath not given us the spirit of fear, but of power, and of love, and of a sound mind" (II Timothy 1:7). This scripture suggests that fear is not from God and that it imprisons us in a world unto ourselves—a world filled with negativity and darkness, shutting out love from others while stifling our emotional, physical, mental, and spiritual growth.

Hypnosis has the capability to empower those who embrace it. It enables us to use our minds to conquer our weaknesses, fears, and uncertainties, as well as that sense of helplessness we may have.

What we dream, we can believe; what we believe, we will become.

Accepting this philosophy can result in the loss of our fears, those fears being replaced by a spirit of power, which frees us to love confidently and with sound mind. Hypnosis has the potential to move us toward a more peaceful, productive, and meaningful life.

As the West developed new knowledge of science, it looked for physical methods of treating illnesses. Scientists discounted the use of hypnosis, as they could not effectively measure its success or explain how it worked.

In the mid eighteenth century, an Austrian doctor, France Anton Mesmer, brought hypnosis back into the medical community. Mesmer believed that a magnetic field surrounded the body and that he could affect a patient's health by manipulating this force field. He developed clinics that consisted of huge open-air baths accompanied by soft music. In the evenings, while patients soaked in the tubs, Mesmer would appear, wearing long, flowing white gowns, purple capes, and large necklaces with pendants of the moon and stars around his neck. He seemed to be a hundred years ahead of the California hot-tub craze. This setting, combined with his skill as a showman, had people quickly reach their expectation and slip into a trance, coining the term *mesmerize*. Mesmer's reputation and success as a doctor grew, and soon people lined up at his door. He even became a court physician for Louis XVI, but he could not keep up with the public demands for his services, so he claimed to have magnetized trees in front of his home, where people could come and heal themselves.

His reputation attracted the attention of several well-known people of the time, including Benjamin Franklin, who formed a group to look into the truth of Mesmer's theories. They reported that, in their opinion, there was no truth to the magnetic fields and that the recoveries of the patients were solely the results of their own minds and imaginations. The committee had uncovered the secret of his success but had failed to really see it. Through hypnotic suggestion and expectation, Mesmer had people healing themselves, but instead of honoring the breakthrough, they branded him a fraud, and he fled discredited. History records Mesmer as the modern discoverer of hypnosis.

Hypnosis continued to develop as a form of entertainment, but the medical community largely ignored it until an English physician, Dr. John Elliotson, began to study the work of Mesmer and use it on his own patients. Elliotson used hypnosis effectively as an anesthetic during surgery, finding that his patients felt no pain.

In India, a Dr. James Estalle was performing similar operations. He too found that once patients entered a trance he could perform major surgery on them without the use of any other anesthesia.

In 1840, Dr. James Braid began researching the work of his fellow physicians and discovered that the trance-like state resembled sleep. He found that while subjects were in this state, they were susceptible to suggestions. Braid called the state *hypnosis,* deriving the term from the Greek word *hypos,* meaning "to sleep." His later research convinced him it was not truly a state of sleep, so he tried to correct his earlier mistake by changing the name to *monoidysm.* The original word stuck, however, and we still call the state *hypnosis* even though it is widely acknowledged that it has nothing to do with sleep.

In 1892, the British Medical Association formally recognized hypnosis as a medical tool. However, it was not widely used until World Wars I and II, when it was utilized to help patients suffering from shell shock or during operations in which there were no anesthetic supplies.

Despite many recorded and amazing uses of hypnosis in the field, modern medicine overlooked hypnosis as an option as it became fascinated with drugs and new technology. It was not until Dr. Milton Erickson began experimenting with hypnosis during the 1940s and 1950s that the medical community gave it a second look. In 1958, the American Medical Association joined in deciding that hypnosis was an important medical tool, but it tried to limit its practice to its own members.

Today, hypnosis is used as an effective method for weight loss and is recognized as the easiest way to stop smoking. Occasionally, hypnosis serves as an anesthetic, and many psychologists use it to assist patients in overcoming fears and phobias.

Largely because of its image in the movies and the misconceptions surrounding it, hypnosis has still not gained wide acceptance, so in some areas, such as sports, in which hypnosis is used to improve focus and mental training, it is done under different names, such as relaxation or visualization techniques.

Accepted by most of the academic community, practiced by many of the new spiritual movements, and recognized as a way to bring focus and improve the mental side of most sports, hypnosis remains shunned in the corporate world and is used very little aside from in advertising agencies, which already incorporate hypnotic suggestions and techniques into their marketing and advertising programs. Many companies fear that if they offer or use hypnosis, their purposes may be misinterpreted and they will be accused of controlling or programming either their employees or clients. As sports are often used as a metaphor for business and as more of the leading athletic heroes of the day admit to using hypnosis to improve their game, some of the larger corporations are beginning to see how it can benefit them, their employees, and their clients.

One large financial institution suggested that if I dropped the word *hypnosis* from my book and put in *visualization techniques*, they would promote it and have me speak at their conference—but they believed that people were too sensitive to the word *hypnosis*.

After banging my head against the wall for some time trying to break back into the corporate world I had spent most of my life in, I was ready to join in and change focus. Then, while teaching a sales training session with Myrna, she connected some of what we were teaching with what I was doing for other individuals through hypnosis. The company we were presenting to was one of the five largest in the country, and one of the VPs there wanted to explore the idea of using hypnosis further. This leader had the insight to say that it didn't matter whether the improvements were personal or career-related, that any improvement a person makes reflects positively in the workplace. Therefore, the company's managers were given instructions that they could visit me for any reason, which would be known only by the participants and me, and that the company would pay for the sessions. Before long, I had hypnotized a couple dozen managers on everything from stopping smoking and addressing a lack of confidence to soothing fears about selling and setting more effective goals. These middle managers reported great results, and soon they were referring other very conservative corporations to also have me hypnotize their employees.

When a person looks at the stress, pressure, and competitiveness today's work force has to contend with, why wouldn't a corporation do as professional athletic organizations do and build a program to improve the mental game of its team?

five

What Is Hypnosis?

The Law of Values states that *you always act in a manner consistent with your innermost values and convictions. What you say and do, the choices you make—especially under stress—are an exact expression of what you truly value, regardless of what you say.*

We discovered earlier that hypnosis is a natural state of consciousness, which most people already experience several times during the course of a day. It has been described as a heightened state of awareness in which the mind becomes focused on something to the exclusion of all else.

Most of us may not be aware of how easily we slip in and out of hypnotic trances. But how often have you gotten into your vehicle to drive to the store and ended up at your office, your house, or some other place you did not intend to go? Often I would drive for miles on northern highways only to realize suddenly that I did not know where I was. I knew approximately where I was, but I could not remember if I had passed a certain town or point in the road or not. I believed that it was simply because I was daydreaming, but in fact, I was driving while in a hypnotic trance. The only reason I was able to drive well while not paying attention and not end up in an accident was that I was operating using two streams of consciousness. The subconscious was driving while the critical-thinking conscious mind was totally engaged in thinking of something different. I am sure that you too can think of similar examples in which you operated almost unconsciously or in a trance-like condition and were unaware of what was happening around you.

We often enter a hypnotic trance while watching a movie or TV. Advertising executives know the value of communicating with viewers in this condition and often try to give suggestions to our subconscious by linking their products to messages that appear to be quite different than what the commercial mainly seems to be saying. For example, beer commercials often say very little about the quality, taste, or cost of their products. Instead, they show a group of very attractive young people having fun, laughing, and bonding with each other, along with images of the label, logo, and packaging colors. Through the effective use of indirect suggestion, the message the beer companies are sending to the subconscious is simply this: if you want to look good, stay young, and have a great time with good friends, drink our brand of beer.

While viewers are in a hypnotic state, their critical-thinking ability is suspended and their critical-thinking conscious mind does not evaluate the messages. They may believe they are not paying attention to the ad or that it has no real effect on them. They may not even remember the brand name; however, the next time they are in the store and about to buy beer, they find they are attracted to the same brand and packaging shown in a commercial and will begin to experience some of the same good feelings they were exposed to in the ads.

That is crazy, you say. It is interesting that the entertainment industry claims that movies only reflect our social values but do not set or influence them. It defends its right to portray violence and other widely unacceptable behavior as entertainment because, it claims, the movies in no way influence the viewers to engage in similar activities. It states that the reason an American citizen is five to ten times more likely to be murdered than a European has nothing to do with the larger number of violent TV shows or movies Americans watch.

This same industry has successfully sold product placement in the James Bond movie *Die Another Day* for over $100 million. James Bond drove an Aston Martin in his older movies but switched to a BMW for *GoldenEye* in 1995. BMW claimed their sales of that particular sports car, the Z3, skyrocketed. Ford, which now owns Aston Martin, brought it back as Bond's car of choice in 2002, with numerous Fords in place as the co-stars' cars. In each movie, Q gives Bond a special new Omega watch, his shirts are Turnbull and Asser, his razor is a Spectra, he flies only British Airways, and he still likes his martinis shaken, not stirred—though now with a different brand of vodka. Recently, Smirnoff stated that the demographics of Bond fans no longer fit its customer profile, so Bond changed his vodka to Finlandia, though he still enjoys his old favorite, Dom Perignon champagne, served at 38 degrees Fahrenheit.

The list goes right down to his sunglasses, the soft drinks served, and the makeup the Bond girls wear. Why are these companies spending millions of dollars to have their products appear in these movies? The answer is simple. In a hypnotic state (relaxed and focused), you are open to indirect suggestions and will link one thing with another. When a viewer sees James Bond using these products, the message that is being linked is that in order to have an exciting life and have beautiful women throw themselves at you, drink Finlandia vodka, drive a BMW or an Aston Martin, wear what James wears, use what James uses, consume what James consumes. The entertainment industry has obviously convinced large companies to part with millions of dollars because they believe the power of suggestion really works when it comes to selling products—although it will not make viewers more violent or antisocial.

If you are male and have ever watched a movie with a good car chase in it, you will remember how hard it was to drive sensibly when the film was over. Did the movie have a hypnotic effect on you? Which of the industry's opposing stories do you believe?

Equally important is what hypnosis is not. As I have repeatedly stated, hypnosis is not mind control. Many classic movies feature an evil villain with shifty eyes, a handlebar moustache, and a pocket watch who takes control of the pretty heroine's mind and keeps her under his spell using hypnosis. This may have made a good story, but it is not possible, for two reasons.

First, if you will recall, all hypnosis is self-hypnosis, so you will only allow yourself to be hypnotized if you want to be hypnotized. No one can hypnotize you against your will.

Second, extensive research and experiments have shown that people will not carry out suggestions under hypnosis that they would not carry out consciously. In cases in which subjects are given a suggestion that is in conflict with their morals or ideals, they normally terminate the trance. This is one reason the industry feels it is not shaping our culture but only reflecting it. However, many experts argue that any message repeated often enough will eventually be accepted as the truth. Repetition is that much more powerful in hypnosis, and so the child who watches the eight thousand murders on TV that he is exposed to by the time he finishes elementary school can be influenced into believing violence is an acceptable reaction.

So if you will not do things you do not want to, what about last year, when the hypnotist came through town and your Uncle Charlie got up on the stage and began to quack like a duck?

Stage shows are designed to create or support the illusion that the hypnotist has complete control over the participants. The truth is, Charlie had a desire to be part of the performance when he volunteered to go up onstage. He knew he would be asked to do things that would make people laugh, yet mentally he agreed to give the hypnotist the power over his mind in order to serve that desire. As long as no suggestion that conflicted with his values was given to him, chances are he would comply.

The stage hypnotist normally begins by asking for volunteers, and several people come forward. During the induction, the hypnotist watches the volunteers, sending several back down to their seats and leaving only about 25 percent of the people onstage. This gives some the impression that they are not hypnotizable or that many people cannot be hypnotized. It is not that the people sent back down could not be hypnotized, it is just that only 10 to 15 percent of the population will go to a deep level very quickly, and those are the people the stage hypnotist is looking for.

Once hypnotized, the subjects look unconscious, but they are completely aware of what is going on around them. They have control and can hear, see, feel, smell, taste, and speak. They will remember everything that happens unless they receive a suggestion of amnesia. The difference between being in a state of hypnosis and consciousness is that if the people under hypnosis receive a suggestion that is morally reasonable, does not conflict with their values, and pleases them, they are likely to accept it. They may do this despite the fact that, under ordinary conscious circumstances, they would consider it an impossible suggestion.

Because people remember everything, and because they were not requested to do the funky chicken in the office, many hypnotherapy clients feel they are not able to enter the suggestive state of hypnosis. It is important for new clients to understand what hypnosis is so that the session meets their expectations.

One of my first clients was a young woman who visited me to help her quit smoking. After the session, she believed that she had not been hypnotized and began to apologize profusely for not being able to let go and reach a level of hypnosis. I said that I thought she had and suggested that she give it a week before we scheduled another appointment. At the end of the week, we accidentally met at the wedding dance of a mutual friend, and she immediately began apologizing again for not being able to enter hypnosis. I asked how she was doing, and she said she had not smoked all week but saw nothing unusual in that, as she had gone that long before. I suggested we give it some more time before booking another appointment.

I didn't hear from her again, so I called her three months later to see how she was doing. She immediately began saying, "I feel so bad that you weren't able to hypnotize me, Layton," and she continued apologizing a third time for not being able to be hypnotized. She then added that she would not be booking another session, as she decided after seeing me at the dance that if she could go for a week without smoking, why not just quit on her own?

I ran into her again two years later, and she said she had not experienced a craving or desire to smoke but still felt it was just a coincidence that she decided to quit the same day I had failed to hypnotize her.

We talked about it, and it became clear the problem was that I had not met her expectations. She didn't know exactly what she should have experienced, but she felt it should be something magical. She thought she should have lost any memory of the session or felt something very strange and uncontrollable take place, but all she had felt was a deep, comfortable state of relaxation.

The subconscious mind remains a mysterious thing, but we know it is capable of incredible feats. We understand how we can change the beliefs held by the subconscious mind through hypnotic suggestion and thereby change results.

Research supports the argument that proper hypnotic techniques are the keys to unlocking the incredible power in our subconscious minds. I say proper use of hypnotism because learning to assist people in entering into a hypnotic state is easy. It is the forming and delivery of an effective suggestion while they are in the hypnotic trance that is the challenge.

The key to achieving successful change is in the message the sub-conscious mind hears, not only while in a hypnotic state but anytime our conscious mind is giving it orders or instructions, either verbally or mentally.

six

Did You Hear What You Said?

The Law of Mind states that *all causation is mental. Your thoughts become your realities. Your thoughts are creative. You become what you think about most of the time. Think continually about the things you really want, and refuse to think about the things you do not want.*

The most important part of the process is the manner in which the hypnotist communicates with or addresses the subconscious mind once a person has entered a hypnotic state. We will explore what we say, as well as how to say it best in the language of the subconscious mind.

One of my first clients was training to run a half-marathon. The birth of her children seemed to have had an undesirable effect on her bladder control, and she often worried that she might not be able to run the full distance without requiring a stop. During a ten-kilometer race she had run, she felt she could not hold on, and the pressure forced her to quit short of the finish line to look for a restroom. She discussed the problem with her doctor, who told her about an operation she could undergo that could eliminate it. The doctor told her it was not an easy operation and suggested that if she wanted to continue distance running without surgery she should consider using Depends or some other way of dealing directly with the problem. My client did not feel that this was an acceptable solution, so she decided on using a hypnotic suggestion, which she dubbed "the case of mind over bladder."

After entering a light trance, I gave her the suggestion that in the future she would easily make it to the finish line. During the next race, the thought of needing a bathroom never entered her mind, and she easily ran the distance. However, the subconscious mind takes commands literally and does not reason or evaluate new beliefs; it simply stores them, holds them, and acts on them. So, when she reached the finish line, the old feeling suddenly hit her without warning, and harder than before. She was almost in a state of panic as she ran knock-kneed for the nearest bathroom, chanting, *mind over bladder, mind over bladder.* "It was horrible," she said. "I was in a panic. I almost didn't make it." We subsequently changed the suggestion, and the difference in the new language of the specific instructions worked. She now often runs in races—even half-marathons—without a problem, going the full distance plus some safe additional time before requiring a restroom.

I told this story to an experienced hypnotist, who then relayed a number of stories about how the language we use affects our subconscious. One story was of a young woman who had begun a great singing career, but each time she was booked for an important engagement, she would begin to gain weight. She tried to control her weight with diet, but the problem would persist until the engagement passed, and then within a short period of time her weight would return to where it had been before.

She visited a hypnotherapist and found that she had been telling her subconscious for years that her goal was to become a "big star." Her subconscious mind interpreted that to mean that she should get bigger before performing. Once the language used in the suggestion to the subconscious was changed, this problem went away.

Affirmations and goal-setting statements are waking hypnotic suggestions, and the key to the formation and the language used contains the same three principles: positive language, first person, and present tense.

Good statements use positive language because the subconscious mind thinks and remembers in pictures, and there are no pictures of negatives. In other words, if you close your eyes and I suggest that you do not think about the Eiffel Tower, what do you see? Most people will see the Eiffel Tower, because there is no defined picture of "not the Eiffel Tower." Smokers know this all too well, because most can go a considerable length of time without smoking if their mind is preoccupied with something else, but as soon as they see a nonsmoking sign, the message they visualize is, "Hey, it's time for a smoke." Therefore, a suggestion of "Do not smoke" only registers as "Smoke, smoke, smoke."

In fact, every parent knows this to be true with kids. What seems to happen right after you tell a youngster not to spill the milk? The more you tell them they cannot or should not do something, the more they seem inclined to do it. The message is negative, so the mental picture they get is the positive—one of spilling milk. For this reason, it is important to think about the outcomes you *do* want, not those you do not want.

Hypnotic suggestions, like good affirmations, are made in the first person. Clients are instructed to repeat "I" in their minds, as in, "I see myself at my ideal weight and shape."

Statements or suggestions delivered also become more powerful if formed in the present tense. In other words, state the desired outcome as though it has been achieved. In the suggestion above for weight loss, for example, the client is instructed to see him or herself at the desired or ideal weight and shape, as opposed to suggesting that he or she will *become* the ideal weight or shape. At no time would a negative statement such as "I will not gain more weight" be acceptable.

Make notes of the language or words you use while describing your goals, and use those same words in the suggestion. This is important, because words are only a representation of something, not the actual thing, and everyone attaches an emotion to words. Suggestions are more powerful if they have a strong emotional attachment, and the way to ensure that is to use the right words. For example, the words "the chair" are neutral to most of us; however, if our fondest memories are cuddling up with a parent in a big recliner known as "the chair," those words will trigger warm emotions. On the other hand, if you had to sit on a hard wooden chair for punishment as a child, the emotion triggered by those words will be negative. In extreme cases, if someone close to you was sentenced to execution in "the chair," the negative emotions would be supercharged.

If simple words like "the chair" can trigger such a wide range of emotion, think how important more complex or emotionally loaded words can be in a suggestion. Because someone else gets a certain emotion from a certain word does not mean it will trigger the same response in you, so the safe way to form a suggestion for yourself is to use the same words in the same context as you do while talking about your goals.

These principles of successful suggestions and statements will be dealt with in more detail in the goal-setting chapter as well.

seven

What's Up, Doc?

The Law of Subconscious Mind states that *your subconscious mind makes all your words and actions fit a pattern consistent with your self-concept and your innermost beliefs about yourself.*

Your subconscious mind will move you forward or hold you back depending on how you program it.

A hypnotherapist can assist a client in making incredible changes; however, hypnosis should be used in conjunction with, not as a substitute for, medical attention. You should proceed with hypnotherapy only after confirming that you are not covering or masking a serious medical problem. Hypnotism is only a tool, but it is a powerful tool, so use it wisely and be careful whom you allow to practice on you.

Hypnotism is not a replacement for therapy or conventional medicine. In the hands of a professional counselor, hypnotherapy can overcome deep-seated problems. Used in conjunction with medical professionals, it can assist in treating a number of serious medical concerns, but if used in these fields by an untrained person, it can add to the problem. For example, hypnosis is very effective in relieving pain, but only under the direction of or with the approval of a doctor.

One area in which hypnosis is used frequently for pain control is the field of dentistry. When my oldest son, Carson, was five, he had a cavity that needed to be filled. We had talked to him about what the dentist would do, and he was looking forward to it. But as Myrna was taking him out the door, our well-intentioned nanny said, "Don't worry about the needle, they don't hurt." Two negatives in this case did not make a positive, and in his mind he heard, "Worry about the needle, they hurt." He would not open his mouth once in the office, and after several minutes of trying, our frustrated dentist suggested we book another appointment. We took Carson to a hypnotherapist, who gave him a suggestion and triggered it with his favorite word, "hockey." She suggested that when we take him back to see the dentist a second time, we should coach the dentist to talk hockey with him. The dentist met him in the waiting room and asked him about his favorite sport, then led him to the chair, where he continued to talk about hockey while filling the cavity with no resistance at all from Carson. Ten years later, Carson still has never had a problem seeing a dentist.

Hypnotism has also served as a powerful anesthetic during serious surgery, including amputations, so it makes sense that seeing a hypnotherapist to rid ourselves of a source of constant pain makes good sense. The problem is that pain is the body's way of telling us there is something wrong with it. A hypnotic suggestion that eliminates pain may hide a serious developing medical problem until it is too late for a doctor to effectively deal with it. Use hypnotic suggestions that deal with medical problems only after consulting a physician.

The same is true for people dealing with serious mental disorders. Suggestions that deal with problems requiring ongoing counseling should be taken only in cooperation with a professional counselor. Sometimes it is difficult to know if a problem is severe enough to require professional help. In those cases, the rule is simple: if in doubt, consult a doctor.

Beware that what appears to be a simple problem may often in fact be the result of something much more complex. This is common when dealing with weight control. In the past, we viewed weight issues as a simple mathematical formula stating if the calories consumed are more than the calories expended, there will be weight gain, and vice versa. Dr. Atkins has since shown that this is not the case and that the type of calories plays a huge role in weight control.

Hypnosis can be a very effective way of dealing with weight, as it can change our core beliefs about food and eating. However, there may be medical reasons why a person is overweight and should not limit his or her diet or begin a new, rigorous exercise program. Again, do not proceed without first checking with a doctor, especially if the weight loss desired exceeds 25 percent of body weight.

Over the years, I have found that almost half of the clients who came in for weight control had a weight problem because of some deeper issue. As such, weight control is also an area in which hypnotherapists can quickly find themselves drawn into issues that exceed their expertise.

There is a franchise currently using hypnosis effectively to help people lose weight. My concern is that they also run a school teaching the simple art of hypnosis—not hypnotherapy—and the students who are studying how to hypnotize people do so on the weight-loss clients with little or no training on other issues. It seems similar to paying full price to have your hair done in hairdressing school—only you risk more than a nick in the ear.

The big issues people with weight problems have include self-confidence. They are fearful of something and unconsciously build a wall around their inner self for protection.

This is particularly true of women who suffered physical, verbal, or sexual abuse as children. Growing up, they became nervous about relationships or men in general, and so, to ward them off, they added a layer of unattractive fat. Many of the women I have counseled for weight loss told me that they feel they added weight for similar reasons when they were younger and now that they are mature, they have a problem losing it. Even though they are older and understand at a conscious level that this is an illogical reason, the subconscious mind is not rational and may hold onto the core belief, thinking it is still protecting them.

Attractive women often add pounds in order to deflect attention from their physical beauty. One such very attractive slim woman had always graduated at the top of her class. She graduated from college and began her own business. When she started her business, she wanted people to know that she was successful because of how smart she was, not because of how good-looking she was, but people often commented on her looks instead of her business acumen. A few years later, she began gaining weight, and although she tried numerous diets over the years and took up running, she could not shake the pounds off. For three years, she ran five to ten kilometers per day, three or four days per week, but still she did not lose weight. Then, suddenly, the pounds began to melt away and she lost several sizes.

When I questioned her about what had changed, she said, "Nothing. I no longer diet, and my routine is the same." Then she admitted to a change in thinking, which she was embarrassed to share at first.

The woman told me that one night near her birthday, she was contemplating her life when this thought suddenly popped into her mind. She thought that now that she was in her mid-forties and had been in business for years, it would be acceptable to be both successful and attractive.

She said that although she had not consciously planned to put on the weight, once her thinking changed, the weight just went away.

The illogical subconscious mind is very powerful, and once it grabs onto an idea that it believes is somehow serving or protecting us, it is very difficult to shake it.

The suggestions below are from well-meaning parents who used food as a reward:

- "Be a good boy (or girl) and you will get a cookie."
- "Clean your plate and you can have dessert."

Later, every time people who have heard these suggestions feel that they deserve a reward for doing well or that they need to be comforted, they feed the feeling.

On the other hand, if things are not going well, they may attempt to console themselves with a reward anyway. Either way, win or lose, they eat more than they should, because it makes them feel good.

Other parents use guilt to get children to eat properly, so they tell them they have to clean their plates before they leave the table because there are "starving kids in (pick your favorite Third World country)." Unless your parents were planning to mail the leftovers to these starving kids, there is no relationship between throwing food away and them starving. However, the link has been made at a subconscious level, and now whenever you do not clean your plate, you get a guilty feeling that somewhere someone is starving—and it is your fault. The person may no longer even make the connection but just remember or trigger the guilt feeling without knowing why, so to avoid it, many of us dutifully clean our plates. Some of us go even further as we clean up the dishes after the meal, finding a spoonful of this or that that is too little to save in the refrigerator and so eating it as well.

Again, the core belief does not have to make logical sense to the subconscious mind; it owns the program and responds accordingly.

The list of reasons people are overweight is long, and often the real reason is buried so deeply that even the client is no longer aware of it, requiring more than one appointment before that reason comes to the surface.

I remind clients that the subconscious mind's number one objective is to protect the body, and it holds onto suggestions in the belief that it is somehow serving that purpose. I then ask them, "If you could go into your mind and knock at the door of the subconscious and ask it, 'How is my being this way serving me?' how do you think it would answer?" Of course, often their response is that it doesn't. "It doesn't serve me to be overweight, it doesn't serve me to smoke, and everyone knows that, it doesn't serve me to . . . " Whatever the issue is, it doesn't serve them.

Sometimes they even become a little annoyed with the question, but just as often the answer immediately slips out. When it doesn't, I follow that first question with a second one: "If you did know, what do you think the answer would be?" It is amazing how often the answer comes to the conscious mind and how, when you think about it without analyzing or rationalizing, it makes sense why the subconscious mind would hold that belief.

The woman with a very attractive face or smile who carries an extra fifty pounds suddenly blurts out that she did not like the unwanted attention she got as a young woman or that eating makes her feel good. Fear of public speaking prevents the otherwise successful man from being laughed at, and a fear of cold calling removes the risk of rejection.

I asked this question of a sixty-three-year-old bus driver, and when he could not identify a reason he could not stop smoking, I suggested that often people begin the same habit for one of two opposite reasons. The first is that they just want to fit in with their friends, be accepted by others, or become a part of the crowd. The second is that they want to stand out from the crowd and make a rebel statement. They see themselves as a pouting James Dean with a cigarette dangling out of his mouth. They see smoking as saying, "I am in control of my life, I do as I please, I am independent, and I am free," or some other statement of defiance. When I asked him what his reason was, the older fellow began to laugh and said he was definitely the rebel. He then relayed how in his day a teacher could strap a student for smoking on school grounds but had no authority off the school property, so he would purposely stand across from the school and smoke. As the teachers arrived, he would call their names and wave to them, cigarette in hand, so they would see him.

The bus driver stopped, and then said, "I'm sixty-three years old. You don't think I still want to be the rebel, do you?"

I said, "I don't know. What do you think?"

He laughed and said that a year before, the rules had changed to prohibit anyone from smoking on the bus, but the union agreements allowed the drivers to stop for a five-minute smoke break every hour. If he had a charter of nonsmokers, they would sometimes get on his case, so he would light up as he stepped off the bus so that the passengers would have to step through the smoke if they got off. He laughed again and said, "You know, I do think there is still a little rebel left inside."

We addressed it by having him see himself as a slave to the large tobacco companies that were taking advantage of him and thinking that he would really be a free and independent person if he were smoke-free. In this way, he was able to let go of this symbol of defiance and finally quit the habit.

This model worked so well that I began using it often. Then just recently it backfired on me. Today, tobacco companies are portrayed in the media as the largest and most heartless, ruthless big businesses on the planet. Playing to this mass perception and having people see how in their quest to be independent they have in fact become the opposite—a slave to the tobacco companies—worked well for me until Ellen visited me.

Her first session was unsuccessful, and just before beginning an induction for her second session, I asked if there was anything else I should know. She said, "This may sound silly, but I am a stockbroker, and when you talked about breaking free of the large tobacco companies, my mind reminded me that I carry a lot of their stock in my portfolio and that if everyone began to think this way, the value would plummet. Given the size of these tobacco companies, this could be disastrous for the stock market." Suddenly, her stopping smoking was about to cause the collapse of the free market system as we know it. Illogical, yes; not rational, yes; silly even—but a belief in her subconscious mind that was preventing her from achieving her conscious goal.

The point is, choose a qualified hypnotherapist who is prepared to deal with more than just what appears on the surface. There may be nuggets of information lying on the surface, but the real gold is found by digging for it.

eight

Does Your Left Brain Know What Your Right Brain Is Doing?

The Law of Subconscious Activity states that *as soon as the subconscious mind accepts any idea, it immediately begins trying to put it into effect. It uses all its resources to that end. It uses every bit of knowledge that you have ever collected, most of which you have totally forgotten, to bring about its purpose. It mobilizes the many mental powers that you possess, most of which you never consciously use. It lines up all the laws of nature as they operate both inside and outside of you to get its way.*

If the idea is difficult, your subconscious mind will still bring about success; if it is impossible, it may take a little longer, but you will be amazed at the results you get. Most great accomplishments were considered impossible at one time.

This law pertains to both good and bad ideas—the subconscious does not judge. When used negatively, it brings sickness, trouble, and failure; when used positively, it brings healing, freedom, and success.

The conscious mind gives the orders, and the subconscious mind does the work.

We know we are most susceptible to suggestions when we are in a hypnotic state, and we know that we are in and out of this state a number of times every day. We also know that our ability to visualize or imagine things in our minds makes the accepting of a hypnotic suggestion easier.

The old myth of the weak-minded being more susceptible is in fact the opposite of reality. The more intelligent and creative a person's mind is, the more control that person will have over it, and the easier it will be to enter a hypnotic state.

We know that prestigious suggestions are easier to accept because they come from someone we give authority or power to. If the doctor you trust suggests that you only have three months to live, the mind accepts it and the doctor's prediction becomes unbelievably accurate. That is why we must be careful of messages given to us by people we look up to, whether they are judges, policemen, lawyers, actors, rock stars, or parents. Doctors, who hold possibly the highest level of esteem in our culture, can administer powerful prestigious suggestions.

We know that children are in and out of the hypnotic state more often than adults are, and the fact that children have better imaginations makes it easier for them to visualize a desired outcome. Children also give more credence to higher authorities than adults do. For example, all first- or second-grade students think their teacher is one of the smartest people in the world. As adults, we often see first- and second-grade teachers as young adults with a number of issues of their own, but as children we saw them as all-knowing.

Suppose one day a young second-grade teacher came to class after enduring a sleepless night because she just broke up with her boyfriend. Tired and stressed, she gives a spelling test. One young student fails miserably yet again—not because he is not bright but because he again failed to look at the assignment. The teacher looks at the test and then throws it back on the desk in frustration, saying, "You will never get this right! I don't think you will ever learn to spell." The child takes this new belief directly to his subconscious and as a result spends a lifetime struggling with spelling.

Every time a new long or difficult-looking word comes up, this young person's inner voice says, "There is no sense trying to remember that one. You are a bad speller and you won't get it right anyway." The thought creates the action, which is to not pay attention to the word, and the result is that the person doesn't learn to spell it properly. My wife, Myrna, on the other hand, somehow got the suggestion that she is among the world's best spellers. When she hears a new word or difficult name she has not heard before, she will stop the conversation and ask for the correct pronunciation. She will then sound it out and ask how it is spelled. She even often asks where the word came from or what it means exactly. By the time she is done, she knows the word and will be able to spell, say, and use it correctly in the future. Her thoughts create different actions than the second-grade student's thoughts created, which generates different results. I can be a part of that same conversation as my wife and watch the process she goes through, yet I do not get the same results. I am often listening to my inner voice reminding me that I was that first young person, which makes me believe that I could never learn to spell a word that difficult.

Even when young people are right, they will doubt themselves long after they forget the original remark and the teacher who planted it in their subconscious.

So, what suggestions are planted deep in your mind?

Remember the story about how I could not stand up and speak in class and would often say it was because I was afraid I would not remember my name? I used that expression for years, but it was not until a few years ago that I linked the expression and my fear to a specific incident. I always remembered this incident but had never made the connection between the two. The fact that I remembered the incident so clearly should have led me to realize some time ago the powerful effect it had on me.

There was no preschool or kindergarten in my town when I was young, so when I entered first grade none of the students knew how to read. I could write my name in capital letters, but that was all. The teacher would have us all open our books and follow along word by word as she read to us. One day she stopped and said, "Someone here knows this next word." I looked around to see who the smart kid was, but no one seemed to know. She insisted that someone should know it, but I could see that no one did. Then the teacher looked at me and said, "Layton, the word is *park*. That is your last name." And everyone laughed at me.

I had never seen my last name spelled in lowercase letters before. As far as I was concerned, it might as well have been written in Chinese. But for the next twelve years, I was afraid to speak for fear of not knowing my own name and having everyone laugh at me. Even the link was there in my own words, but I did not know why I was so afraid.

These types of events can be revisited and treated using regression therapy. Regression therapy coupled with hypnotism takes a person back in time to recall the events or circumstances that affect the way they currently think or what they believe about an issue. Some people go even further back, into what they believe are past lives, feeling that they can access those memories and make changes in their minds that will affect their current situation.

Some cultures believe in past lives and some don't. Although I do not use past-lives techniques in my practice, I feel it is not my place to judge or question my clients' beliefs. If they believe that accessing a past life will help them in the present, who am I to say they are wrong? Therapy sessions are all about the clients and what it will take to assist them in living healthier, fuller lives now and in the future.

Hypnotism is effective in reframing past events or how we have viewed ourselves in the past so that we can see things from a different perspective. We already understand that we are a reflection of the way we see ourselves. Change the picture inside and the results will change on the outside.

It is beneficial to understand the relationship between the brain and the power of the subconscious mind. The brain has two halves, referred to as the left brain and the right brain. Most people understand that the left brain is the logical, analytical side where we do most of our critical thinking. People who tend to favor using this side of the brain often enter careers such as engineering, accounting, computer programming, and others that follow set procedures or use strict mathematical formulas. The right brain is the creative side. It thinks in pictures, and people who favor the right brain often become artists, poets, or people who deal in abstract terms.

I tend to remember which is which by recalling that most of my right-brain friends are often found on the left side of the political spectrum and most of my left-brain friends are found on the right. Go figure!

The two hemispheres of the brain communicate regularly, if not constantly, at the center of the brain, where they are connected. The communication that goes on between the two hemispheres is believed to create our dreams. Dreams and our reason for dreaming are not entirely understood, but dreams are believed to be a part of the processing the brain goes through in sorting and storing information.

The mind seems to occupy both sides of the brain, and it also has two parts. The conscious, logical, reasoning, and critical-thinking part of the mind that we use to carry out our day-to-day activities is believed to reside largely in the logical left side of the brain. The subconscious mind is the largest part of our mind. It carries out all our involuntary activities and holds our long-term memory, and it is believed to reside mostly in the right side of the brain.

I use the words "seems to," "believed," and "mostly" because science has not really nailed down where our mind is. We know that certain areas of the brain control certain functions; however, our mind or spirit cannot be pinpointed with the same degree of accuracy. In fact, there are now a number of theories contending that our mind occupies each cell of our body. There are those who believe that the nerve center in our solar plexus holds some of our intuition abilities, and that is why we refer to "gut" feelings. Others believe there is some truth to the ancient beliefs that the heart holds some of our deepest emotions and that other nerve centers or organs may store some of the functions of our minds. And what about reflex actions, when we don't seem to think but automatically react to given situations we have trained for? Wherever the mind is stored, we do know that the subconscious and conscious minds do work together, yet individually they work very differently.

Each task we learn passes through four phases. The first is what is commonly referred to as the unconscious incompetent. In this phase, we don't know that we don't know. People who have never heard of or seen an automobile may not know that they don't know how to drive one. In the second phase, we are introduced to the new task and discover that we now know that we don't know, and so become a conscious incompetent. Our skill level has not improved but our awareness level has, so we are making progress. With some training and practice, we soon can do the task, as long as we are concentrating on it. Here, we reach the third phase and become a conscious competent. Many of us reach this point in a number of activities and may never pass into the fourth and final phase, that of becoming an unconscious competent. This is where the task has moved from the conscious level to the subconscious level. We no longer have to think about the task; we just do it.

For example, learning to drive begins as a conscious or left-side activity, as we must think about the task in order to execute it. Push in the clutch, shift the gears, step on the gas or the brake, put on the signal lights, turn the wheel, and watch for other traffic. Do you remember how mind-boggling it was the first year you drove an automobile? Then, with practice, it becomes increasingly easier, until many of the functions become an unconscious act, or a right-brain activity. Most of us then become capable of driving for miles with only our subconscious mind awake while our conscious mind daydreams of other things. We often drive in this hypnotic state only to realize that instead of going to our planned destination we end up at another familiar location or simply do not remember driving for some time.

This ability to do one thing at a subconscious level while doing another at a conscious level is really hypnosis. Hypnosis is now defined by many as the ability to concentrate on one thing to the exclusion of all others. Sports figures experience this when they are "in the zone." Athletes have been known to play with intensity while having broken limbs or other serious injuries, completely unaware of the pain. They focus so intently on the game that they don't hear the crowd or see other distractions. It is as though they are on automatic pilot. They have moved their ability to do something from the conscious to the subconscious.

One of the big differences between the conscious and subconscious mind is that the conscious mind is capable of deductive logic whereas the subconscious mind uses inductive logic.

Deductive logic is the process of reasoning from the general to the specific. This means we can make assumptions based on our knowledge of a wide range of experiences and apply it to a single thing or a few things that are similar. For example, if you burn your hand on a candle and then feel the heat of a campfire, you may deduct that flames are hot, and you will tend to avoid sticking your hand on the flames of a gas stove. This is deductive reasoning, or deduction.

Inductive logic is the reverse. With inductive logic, you form generalities from specifics. You may burn your hand on a candle and accept that all candles are hot, then burn your hand on a campfire and accept that all campfires also are hot, and then burn it a third time on the stove and assume that all stoves are hot. Yet you do not make the connection between these events.

The subconscious mind will accept a good suggestion as true if it is repeated often and long enough, because the subconscious mind is not capable of deductive reasoning, even though it is not logical to the conscious mind.

The subconscious mind also houses all of the core beliefs that cause us to act or react in the manner we do. Like the driving skills we discussed earlier, these beliefs resulted from conscious information becoming ingrained into the subconscious.

Even though a belief may not be logical, once accepted by the subconscious mind, it treats the belief as the truth and acts accordingly. The subconscious mind is so powerful that an anorexic person will continue to diet when it makes no logical sense, because in the subconscious mind the person believes he or she has a weight problem and will continue to act accordingly.

The conscious mind is similar to the "desktop" of a computer. Here we review, manipulate, and work on information before storing it in the hard drive, or our subconscious mind. The subconscious mind also stores our long-term memories as well as functions, or programs, that work in the background to keep our operating system going, such as involuntary actions like breathing, heartbeat, and other bodily functions. As we learn repetitive actions, we generate a sequence of electrical impulses, which converts the mental thought into a physical action. These learned responses are stored in the subconscious mind and then recalled as required.

A good example of this transference is typing. As we hear or think of the word we wish to use, we have to face the difficult conscious act of spelling it out, and as we do, we look or remember where each letter is located on the keyboard. With practice and experience, we eventually get to the point at which we just think of a word and it appears on our screen as our subconscious mind both spells it out and our fingers seemingly locate the letters without thought. I recently discussed this with a class, and one woman said if I were to ask where the letter Q was on the keyboard, most typists would have to really think about it—but if I were to let them rest their hands on a keyboard, the little finger of the left hand would automatically go up one space to the letter. We learn to do numerous activities in a similar manner over the course of our lifetime, including walking, running, swimming, cycling, driving, and various sports and household skills that seem to function as an eye-hand response without conscious thought.

By understanding, training, and using our subconscious minds more effectively, we become more competent in the areas we wish to master.

The great hockey player Wayne Gretzky was asked why he excelled at the sport, and he said he didn't follow the puck but went to where it was going to go. When asked how he knew where it was going to go, he said he didn't think about it, he just knew. Years of training and practice had allowed him to take the game to a deeper state, where he trusted his gut feeling and played at a subconscious level.

Using the power of hypnosis, you can train your subconscious mind to respond in a similar manner to almost any task.

nine

The Sporting Life

The Law of Correspondence states that *your life is a reflection of your inner life. There is a direct correspondence between the way you think and feel on the inside and the way you act and experience on the outside.*

Your relationships, health, wealth, and position are mirror images of your inner world.

Many sports figures subscribe to the belief that the mental game is as important as the physical one, yet these same people tend to shudder at the thought of hypnosis and avoid any contact with it. In many sports circles, it is still thought of as mind control, often associated with stage entertainment or considered to be part of the "dark side."

Stage performances are designed to reinforce this negative image. As a result and for that same reason, in some fields, sports especially, hypnosis is referred to by other names, such as visualization.

Recently, a great deal of research has gone into studying the effects of visualization or hypnosis and its outstanding effects on athletic performance.

In the late 1970s, the Soviet Union team began using imagery or visualization practices as part of its training program for the 1980 Olympic Games. It divided its team into four equally matched groups for training purposes. Each of the four groups employed a different training method. The group that trained physically 75 percent of the time and practiced visually 25 percent of the time won the fewest medals. The group that won the most medals at both the summer and winter games practiced their sport visually 75 percent of the time and physically only 25 percent of the time.

The subconscious mind does not differentiate between what is real and what is imagined. This is because the brain fires electrical impulses in the same pattern and frequency when the body is physically rehearsing as it does when practicing the same exercise mentally.

The old adage should say, "Practice does not make perfect, only perfect practice makes perfect." The problem with practicing physically is that it is seldom perfect. It takes a long time to get the movement perfect each time. By practicing mentally through visualization, practice can be perfect from the start. The only movement the athlete practices mentally is the perfect movement. By continuing to practice perfectly in the mind, the athlete quickly sets up a pattern in the subconscious mind, sometimes referred to as a neuron highway, that allows the same actions to be easily repeated physically. This is why the great Jack Nicklaus said, "I don't make a shot that I haven't already practiced in my mind."

This being the case, the only effective way of training for any event is to set up a visualization practice. I have had the pleasure of working with a number of world-class athletes who work on their mental game as seriously as their physical one. Most world-class athletes have access to the same training programs, dietary and nutritional information, equipment, knowledge, effective methods of exercise, and skill drills. Most athletes who compete at a world level have created or shaped their bodies in a similar fashion in order to be the most effective for their particular sport. In fact, if we could somehow measure the top hundred athletes in any specific sport, we would probably find very little difference between the people who are in the top five and those who are in the remaining top ninety-five positions. Despite being almost identical physically to many of their competitors, a small group of athletes dominate every sport and do so consistently.

The key to this is obvious if you listen to them talk about a recent good performance. The language they use has to do with how well prepared they were mentally. They will say things like, "My mental game was on" or "I was mentally prepared," showing that their success was a result of their mental state at the time of the event. It is usually just a small mental edge that separates the winners from the other guys.

Tiger Woods has burned up golf courses around the world and shattered records along the way. He continues to dominate one major event after another, leaving other golfers in awe of him. How does he do it? How can anyone be that much better than the rest of the field?

If you analyze his performance, however, you will find that on average he is usually only one or two strokes per game better than the performance of several other players. This is only 1 to 2 percent better! Most tournaments are made up of four games with a par of 72, for a total par of 288. Most tournaments are won by less than three or four strokes. Four strokes out of 288 is just over 1 percent. How many players on the tour could not improve their performance by 1 percent?

Most players have played at least that much better than their average, but few fail to do so on a consistent basis. It is seldom their mechanical skills that need improving. The ability to be consistent is what needs improvement, and that comes back to the mental game.

In the end, it is not necessarily Tiger's physical skills that make him the dominant player in the world. It is not that Tiger never makes a bad shot, because he does. It is his ability to control his mind and recover from a bad shot that makes him outstanding.

Study the difference between the superstars and the regular players in any other sport and you will find that the difference is always the same. The athlete at the top of the sport usually holds only a small advantage over the field, and often that advantage is not in their physical play but rather in their mental skills.

Hockey offers another excellent example in Wayne Gretzky, as I mentioned at the end of the previous chapter. Several players in the NHL have demonstrated better mechanical skills than Wayne Gretzky did. Wayne was not the fastest skater and he did not have the hardest shot, nor was he the biggest or toughest player. Yet Wayne Gretzky ran away with almost every record in the book and dominated the sport for almost twenty years. Despite the fact that he did not have the best physical skills in the game, most people agree he was one of the greatest players of all time. The difference between Wayne and the other players was his mental game. Wayne focused on what he wanted to do and did not deviate from his plan. As a result, he received few penalties for striking back at the players whose job it was to hassle him constantly. Once, when asked how he kept from retaliating against the constant harassment he faced, he said he would sooner retaliate where it did the most damage: on the scoreboard. He never allowed other players to throw him off his mental game.

Another advantage Wayne may have had has to do with how fast our subconscious mind is able to process information. It seems that we have a survival ability to speed our processor up, making it possible to process the same amount of information in much less time. If you could suddenly process the same information that takes a second to process in half a second, it would appear to your mind as though time had just slowed to half-speed. People talk about experiencing this phenomenon in times of crisis. Perhaps you have experienced it yourself. When people think they are about to die, they report that their entire lives flash before their eyes or that the event itself seems to go in slow motion and time seems to slow down.

Some athletes report that there are times during important performances when they experience a slowing down of the action going on around them and seem to have more time to think and react to what is happening. They refer to this feeling or experience as being in the zone. Some athletes seem to have an ability to control the speed of their subconscious mind and create this illusion that things around them are happening in slow motion.

Being in the zone is the ability to access the subconscious and take advantage of the state it creates. This furthers the argument that the only difference between the top athletes and the also-rans is their use of the subconscious mind.

This same process is transferable to any area of life. Top-producing salespeople mentally rehearse or practice their presentations prior to giving them. They see themselves getting the order or winning the contract while others go with the flow and wonder how it will all shake out. Some Realtors even verbalize it by saying not that they are going to show a house but that they are going to *sell* a house—a subtle but real difference in commands. Remember, the subconscious is a servant that takes its orders literally from the conscious mind. If you are a Realtor about to give an order that you know will be carried out to the letter, would you give the order to go show houses or to sell them? The verbal language you use when instructing your inner mind does make a difference.

The owners and founders of leading businesses regularly explain how they had a vision and clearly saw how their business would unfold while it was still in its infancy.

One story relayed by Art Linkletter told how Walt Disney took him for a drive up to Anaheim in the 1950s, where they walked through an orchard. Walt was looking for investors for a project he had in mind. Mr. Linkletter said that Walt Disney walked him through the orchard, pointing to various areas and telling him how he planned to lay out

Disneyland and what it would look like. He said Walt seemed to be able to see it clearly in his mind's eye as he pointed to where he envisioned Frontierland and where Fantasyland would be located. Art said he looked in the same direction, but all he could see were trees.

Mr. Linkletter said he enjoyed the walk with Walt Disney but declined the offer to invest in a vision he could not see. Art ended the presentation by saying that to the best of his calculations, the walk through the orchard cost him tens of thousands of dollars in lost opportunity for every step he took. He lost the opportunity because he could not see the mental picture or vision that Walt Disney had so firmly set in his own subconscious mind.

People who have the ability to control or program their subconscious mind are the same people who overcome all odds and achieve the visions they create.

The big question is, "How can I learn the same skill?"

My research in this subject continues to lead me back to hypnosis as the key to unlocking the secret. The reason is that hypnosis is the best way to control or program our subconscious mind. Hypnosis does not allow for that mental PS that we all like to tack on to our affirmations.

The hockey player who builds an affirmation that says, "I will be the greatest hockey player in the world" may then add the little PS, "Well, with the exception of Gretzky." In this way, this self-defeating statement or some similar thought programs his own limitations.

ten

May the Force
Be with You

The Law of Creativity states that *whatever your mind can conceive and believe, it can achieve. Every advancement in your life begins with an idea of some kind, and since your ability to generate new ideas is unlimited, your future can be unlimited as well.*

Remember the basic story line of the Star Wars movies? In these stories, the hero, Luke Skywalker, is a Jedi knight, which gives him the ability to mentally access or communicate with the Force. The Force is an energy field that is all-knowing and all-powerful. By accessing this power, Luke is able to battle and eventually defeat the evil dark side.

The concept of the Force or something similar was not new when the first Star Wars movie came out. Variations have been explored and explained, called by numerous names by numerous civilizations, since time immemorial. The entity referred to as the Force in the movie has also been known as the ultimate, infinite, or collective knowledge, the universal or central intelligence, God, the All-Knowing, or one of many other names.

Such a force does exist, and we all have the ability to access it through our subconscious mind. The explanation is simple and does not insult or conflict with any religious beliefs.

Before you close this book and ask to sign the petition to have me committed, bear with me for just a few more pages.

Relax and travel back in time to your grandparents' or great-grandparents' time. A hundred and fifty years ago, much of North America was unsettled, and men were exploring it in canoes, on foot, and on horseback. Outside of the main rail lines in the eastern part of the continent, travel was slow, and a twenty-five-mile trip often took more than a day to complete. The newest communication technology was the telegraph, which could send a short coded message along a wire strung partway across the country. Only a few trained operators understood the series of dots and dashes that clicked on the telegraph keys. Only newspapers carried the news, and the time it took to deliver them ranged from a week to several months, depending on how far they traveled from the source. Compared to the instant communication of news today, it is hard to conceive how society functioned.

Consider what would happen if we traveled back in time to attend a town hall meeting at that time and produced a small plastic radio. The smooth, shiny surface of the plastic box would mystify them, as there was no other material like it then. People would be shocked when they turned the knob on and sound came out. The sound that erupted would startle even the most educated listener.

They would consider it impossible to suggest that this sound came instantly from many miles away and was picked out of thin air by this small box, which had no visible connection to any source. The radio would be unbelievable to them. After the initial shock, it would be considered good news if they laughed and called us crazy, because if it occurred in one of the northeastern states, they could decide to burn us at the stake for practicing witchcraft.

Only three or four generations ago, a portable radio was totally beyond the comprehension of the brightest people of the day. They could not even conceive of how such a thing could be plausible.

Return to today and enter a first-grade classroom. Place the radio on the table along with a small television, a cell phone, a pager, a remote control for any one of a dozen items found around the average home, and numerous other wireless electronic devices.

Tell the six-year-old children that each one of them could have a similar collection of items. Everyone could then dial up and talk to someone else, or listen to or watch a different channel, or operate a different device remotely, all at the same time, all with signals picked out of the same air in their small classroom. Their reaction would be completely different from the first group. "So what's your point?" might be one of the comments from the young, eager children. Another student might even begin explaining how all the equipment works.

So what *is* my point?

My point is that what would have been completely inconceivable to the brightest people of one time period will be generally understood and accepted by children three or four generations later. Who would have believed ten years ago that we would be able to sit down at a personal computer, type out a specific question, send it out into cyberspace, and almost instantly get back volumes of information pertaining to it from who knows where? The Internet is now almost considered a necessity of everyday life. As I sit correcting this manuscript one last time, I decided to type my own name into a search engine, and up popped a link for Amazon advertising this very book. Things happen so fast that they are selling it before I am finished writing it! This idea may have been considered laughable as little as fifteen or twenty years ago. The advancements in technology are incredible.

The theory that I am proposing is similar, and yet to some it will be as unbelievable as the previous examples seemed not that long ago.

The good Lord thought to provide us with everything we needed to make these technologies possible from the very beginning of time. Despite the fact that all of the elements have always been with us, it is only after progressing and evolving for thousands of years that we have reached the knowledge and understanding of how to develop and use these technologies. Are we still so naive as to think that there are not more discoveries that are even more exciting? These discoveries will change the cutting-edge technologies of today into the obsolete telegraphs of the future.

One day we will confirm that the Creator really has provided us with the Force, the central intelligence, the all-knowing power, the energy field, or whatever we choose to call it, and we will then find that we have the capability of accessing it. This mental Internet will allow us to send ideas and thoughts in search of answers. We will receive answers from either the central power or from others who are mentally tuned in to the same frequency. The Internet, as we know it, is only the crude blueprint of what is mentally possible.

Sound crazy? Review what we do know or suspect.

We know we generate brain waves. Modern medicine uses instruments to measure these waves to determine and diagnose health problems. We know that there are a number of different types of waves, which are generated by different mental functions. We know that the type and intensity of these waves changes from sleep to waking and with various other forms of activity.

Suppose for a minute that these waves also carry with them signals or messages, similar in this way to radio waves, which have the ability to be received and interpreted. Just because we cannot do so at this time does not mean it is not possible. Would that not explain mental telepathy, clairvoyance, and other mental phenomena that science currently cannot explain?

We understand that just because a lost tribe from some remote place does not have a radio and cannot receive radio or microwave messages does not mean that those messages do not exist in their area. So who's to say that these mental messages do not exist?

It has been suggested that fish were the last to discover water. When we are completely submerged in something, it is hard to view it clearly from any other perspective. If we are swimming in this pool of information, perhaps, like the fish, we cannot see it from within. It is known that when a fish moves a fin, it sets some water into motion that can be detected by other fish some distance away. From the movement of the water, they know if they should move toward the source or swim away from it. We get similar feelings about some people. We don't know why, but we seem to feel an energy about them that causes us to feel either threatened by them or drawn to them. Is this part of a greater secret we have yet to discover? Are we still at an unconscious incompetent stage in which we are not aware of what we don't know?

We have difficulty understanding this concept when we think that we might be that primitive lost tribe. Just because we currently lack sufficient proof to show that such a system exists does not mean that it does not exist. There is certainly strong evidence that at least supports the possibility that it does exist, and that from time to time our subconscious mind does access this mental Internet. Let me give you just a few examples.

A few years ago, I met a conservative religious man who worked as a minister for the Salvation Army. He told me he had an identical twin brother on the other side of the country. Once, he suddenly awoke from a bad dream in which he had felt a sharp pain in his chest. He said as soon as he got out of bed, the pain subsided, but he knew it meant something was wrong with his brother, whom he had not spoken to in some time. He said that over the years he and his brother had experienced several similar incidents. Within minutes, the phone rang with a message that his brother had suffered a heart attack. Coincidence? Possibly.

Here's another example. At 9:30 p.m. on the first Thursday of June, I finished reading *The Power of Your Subconscious Mind*, by Dr. Joseph Murphy. I put the book down and told Myrna that I had just decided to put into the universe from my subconscious the desire to sell some commercial property we still held in our previous hometown a thousand kilometers away.

I told her how much we would sell it for and suggested that we use the money to buy a home we liked that had just come on the market and was priced for a quick sale. She gave me the same smile that she gives the kids the night the tooth fairy comes. Then she turned out the lights, and we went to sleep. On Friday morning, I got a call from a real estate agent who wanted to know if we would consider selling the same property. I told him that we would, and he said he would show it the next day at noon. The first offer arrived just after lunch on Saturday and was only ten thousand dollars short of the amount I had told Myrna we would accept.

By that evening, less than forty-eight hours after saying I was sending the thought of selling the property into the universe, we had a firm deal at the specified amount with a closing date in only three weeks, almost unheard of for a sale of this type of commercial property. The quickness of the deal allowed us to purchase and close on the house we wanted. Coincidence? Possibly.

Here's one more. Shortly after we moved south, we visited a golf course, and while signing the guest book, Myrna noticed that someone had signed with the same name as a woman she had worked with more than fifteen years before. She said she had not thought of the woman in years and wondered what had become of her. When we went home that evening, she told me she had been thinking of the woman all evening and wondering if the person who had signed the book was the same woman. She looked through the local phone directory, but there was no listing for that name. A few days later, Myrna was reading a regional newspaper and found an article complete with a photo of the woman she knew. The article said she had just started a position in a community about thirty miles away, so Myrna tracked her down through her new place of work. When the woman answered the phone, she said the hairs on the back of her neck stood up because she had not thought of Myrna in the past several years until the same night that Myrna had seen her name in the guest book. She told Myrna that suddenly she had a vision flash through her mind in which she saw Myrna sitting on the floor of her apartment cutting out ads, as she had been doing when she saw her last some fifteen years before. She said she did not know why she would suddenly think of Myrna after all those years, but she did, and when Myrna called a few days later, it really spooked her.

Coincidence? Possibly, but how often has something like this happened to you? I can think of numerous times when I have been thinking of someone and suddenly the phone rings and there they are on the other end. Can you?

Several other examples come to my mind, and I'm sure you have lots as well. How often have you had a vivid dream about some future event which later turned out to be true? What about déjà vu? Is there an explanation for why you suddenly should get the feeling that this has all happened before? Would not the presence of an all-knowing, universal intelligence explain some of these things?

What about goal setting? We know the most powerful way to achieve goals is to create vivid visions of yourself already having reached them. There are a number of theories as to why this works so well, and I will detail them later in the goal-setting chapter. Perhaps one of the reasons is that if you send a vision out onto the mental Internet, the forces conspire to set things in motion, which helps you bring them to fruition.

After fifteen years of teaching other people how to set goals, both Myrna and I are still amazed every time we hear a story similar to the one about selling our property—and we hear them often. Once you change the way in which you set your goals, you will find more of them coming to pass as well.

Clients tell us that once the vision is clear, a door opens or an opportunity appears, and suddenly they achieve their goal. Since it happens with such incredible frequency, we are convinced that whatever guides the process is more than coincidence. I am not a student of the scriptures;

however, it seems to me we are told the secret repeatedly in such verses as, "Knock and the door will be opened." Yet we still do not hear the message.

I believe we can each learn to profit from this amazing power. The scientific community shuns the thought of psychic power and any other strange talk of there being something out there that our subconscious mind may be able to tap into, yet we continue to hear the stories. We often hear of police forces turning to a psychic to provide further clues or leads to follow. Some of my left-brain associates who have been involved in such cases tell me that they do not really believe anyone has such powers. However, they are amazed at some of the things that seem to turn up. Can it all be coincidence?

At some point, sooner or later, a person begins to think that there are just too many coincidences. Is it a coincidence that just about the time someone discovers a new technology, someone else finds the material or a second technology to make it work better? Was it a coincidence that Alexander Graham Bell filed the patent for the first telephone only hours before someone else tried to file a similar one? How often have you had a brilliant and uniquely creative idea only to find that another person has just come up with the same idea? Why did it happen at the same time?

Is it not fascinating that all the elements and all the materials that it takes to make today's wireless communication and the Internet possible have always been with us, but it's only now that the series of discoveries have been made that have allowed us to create the technology? What new events or discoveries await us in the next decade, and where will they lead us? Science reminds us that the universe is balanced, complex, and organized, having its own set of laws, but at the same time was created by a truly amazing set of coincidences that supposedly came from a sudden, seemingly random big bang.

Science has discovered many of the laws of the universe that have been with us since the beginning of time. These are the laws that allow these technologies to work. It is only very recently that collectively we have discovered how to use many of them to our advantage. Perhaps we will soon earn the right to know how to move on to the next step—using the mental laws that will allow us to access the mental Internet.

Science cannot explain why everything is so orderly or why so many of these coincidences continue to reoccur. Science is still trying to discover how the subconscious mind functions and why the power of suggestion, in a hypnotic state, seems to work the way it does. But we know it works, and I believe that within our lifetime we will discover ways of communicating mentally that we cannot even conceive of at this time.

We are all sitting here looking at our minds like the people from a hundred and fifty years ago might have looked at a portable radio. Is such communication impossible just because we have difficulty imagining it? Are our thoughts like the movement of the fish, sending out waves of energy that can be detected at a distance? What thoughts are you sending into the universe? Are they seeking the results you want, or are they attracting the things you don't? The mental sharks will be drawn to you as surely as the results you desire. To be certain, be aware of the messages you are sending, and may the Force be with you, whatever you conceive it to be!

eleven

You Are Only as Sick as You Think You Are

The Law of Concentration states that *whatever you dwell upon grows and expands in your life. Whatever you concentrate upon and think about repeatedly increases in your world. Therefore, you must focus your thinking on the things you really want in your life.*

I have been blessed with good health for most of my life, but I often wonder how much was a random blessing and how much was a result of my mother's constant reminder, "You are only as sick as you think you are. Now get out of bed and go to school." I do not want you to think she was not compassionate, because she was, almost to a fault, but at the same time she just did not allow us to get sick, and because of that, I missed few days of school due to illness.

In my thirty years in the workforce, I do not think I averaged more than one or two missed days per year because of sickness, partly because I have been blessed and partly because I have too many other things to do to be sick.

Mothers often report few "sick days" even when the rest of the family is down with the flu or colds, and when you ask them why that is, they say they just do not have time to be sick because everyone else is counting on them.

Earlier, I discussed the placebo effect and the role that suggestion and hypnosis have played in health. There have been countless studies done on various alternative forms of health care, including the use of faith healers, visualization techniques, yoga, meditation, and various other forms of hypnosis or hypnotic trances to control our own health. This industry is huge and is the subject of numerous books. I will only lightly touch on the subject in this book, in order to demonstrate the power of hypnosis. I have already discussed how the medicine men of old used hypnosis as well as the placebo effect. In both cases, people became well after they thought they had taken something powerful enough to cure them. In these cases, it is generally agreed that it was only the power of their own belief system that cured them, or possibly it was only the power of their own belief system that made them ill in the first place. Either way, it demonstrates the power of the subconscious mind.

With this power in mind, it raises the question of how many death sentences may have been handed out by well-meaning medical providers who told a patient that he or she only had three, six, or twelve months to live and, darn it, were right almost to the day? The chilling thought that comes up is, if the doctor had predicted a year and a half or two years, would the belief system have carried the patient on the extra time? The problem with the mind and doctors is belief. Just like the mysterious medicine man of our ancestors, we hold today's doctors in very high regard and believe most everything they say, because they are so trusted. Belief and trust are powerful forces in the subconscious, and we tend to believe people we give authority to with little question.

One of my heroes is George Burns. For years, George said his goal was to live to be a hundred years old and perform for his birthday. George enjoyed a long and healthy life, but he did not set a goal further out as his birthday approached. It was as though he had told his mind the destination was to live to be one hundred. He turned one hundred years old on January 20, 1996, and then died within two months. I am sure there were medical reasons for his death, but it seems to be a chicken-and-egg story. Did he succumb to his medical problems, or were his final medical problems a result of his mindset, his expectations? Was it just another coincidence that he should live to be a hundred just as he predicted he would, only to die within a very narrow window of having achieved that goal?

Some medical reports suggest that the common flu can be spread visually as easily as any other means. Just seeing people with red eyes and runny noses sneezing, coughing, and generally looking miserable can be enough to trigger symptoms in ourselves. This sparked the debate as to whether the manufacturers of cold remedies know when to advertise the coming flu season or whether the flu season follows the heavy advertising. The general belief is that flu season is in the fall, when the temperature drops and the season turns wet, yet recent studies have shown that neither necessarily increases the incidence of the flu if the body is well rested. This is demonstrated by the number of polar-bear swimmers who take to the water New Year's Day, or the countless other athletes who compete in the wet and cold without catching the flu.

We understand that the most powerful time to plant a suggestion is during a hypnotic or trance-like state, similar to the state we enter while watching TV. The commercial comes on, showing some miserable person with all the visual signs of a cold or flu while a soothing voice-over states with authority that it's time to stock up on supplies, as the flu season will soon be here. To add power to the authority voice, the actor is often dressed to look like a doctor or pharmacist. All the elements of a good hypnotic suggestion are there, and the subconscious mind, the one that does not have reasoning powers, buys the message and tells your body, "Hey, did you hear that? It's time to get a cold."

For this reason, I recommend using self-hypnosis inductions that tell your subconscious you are healthy, feel great, sleep well, and limit who has influence over your thoughts about your wellness.

If you currently have some health challenges, I would suggest that you read all you can find on the subject. Consult your health care provider and use self-hypnotic techniques to reframe some of your current beliefs. Proper inductions will assist with your recovery to the extent that your subconscious mind can affect the problem.

Numerous sources claim to have cured everything from common warts to cancer using hypnosis. While I have no doubt about the power of the mind and understand that we have only just scratched the surface of what we are truly capable of doing, it is important to understand that hypnosis is only the tool, not the cure. Like any tool, hypnosis can be very effective in the hands of a competent practitioner. It can be equally destructive in the hands of one who is not. While many people consider themselves competent at hypnosis, if they are not doctors or medical specialists, they can still assist, but do not substitute them for people who practice medicine. The reverse is also true: a doctor who is not trained in the proper use of hypnosis should not practice it just because he or she is a doctor. It is important to remember that health care professionals are people with similar limitations as the rest of us, and we must be careful to consider the advice they are trained to give about becoming healthier but not buy into their limiting beliefs.

We have all heard stories of people who have made miraculous recoveries or overcome disease or disabilities in cases that the medical community said were impossible. Often the bad news is given for two reasons. One is the health care worker will say that the sooner the patients face the truth, the quicker they can deal with the problem and get on with the rest of their lives or make the appropriate arrangements. The other reason is purely for the health care system's legal protection, trying to keep the patient and family happy, because any positive results are better than what was predicted. Few realize how powerful their prestigious suggestions may be, and it cannot be stressed enough that too many patients buy into these suggestions and help make the predictions come true.

One area of health in which hypnosis is extremely effective is in the relief of stress. We know that a large percentage of today's medical problems, both physical and psychological, arise from stress. The best way to eliminate stress is through the control of our subconscious thoughts, and the most effective way to accomplish that is with the use of hypnosis or self-hypnosis.

Before attacking any health issue, there are two key components to consider: explore what is causing the problem, and take control of it by effecting change in those conditions that are contributing to the cause.

It may require making a change in lifestyle to bring about a cure or avoid future problems. Often, change can be easily accomplished using hypnotic suggestions.

Here's an example. Fred worked hard every day. He was so busy at his desk, handling two phones and dispatching crews, that he seldom had time for a break. Grabbing a coffee or going outside for a smoke was the only way he could get some relief. Time was always an issue, and he took heat from both the crews and the clients keeping him under constant pressure. Fred was happy to get home after work, where he could enjoy his wife's homemade supper. Fred's wife learned to cook on the farm from her mother and knew how to take care of a hungry man: a big helping of meat, mashed potatoes with gravy, buttered vegetables, homemade bread, coffee, and a good dessert. After supper, Fred liked to put his feet up, lie down on the couch with a beer, and relax while watching TV.

Fred worked at the same job for over twenty years and yet it still caused him stress. They rushed Fred to the hospital after he felt extreme chest pains, and the doctor told him he had the onset of heart disease. The news did not come as a surprise to Fred. His dad had died at forty-five from a heart attack. Fred saw no reason to change his lifestyle, as his limiting belief was that he would die early like his father anyway.

Fred was oblivious to the cause of his problem, and he did nothing to take control of it. The unfortunate part is that every day the medical community treats people like Fred, knowing that after they are patched up they will return home to the same lifestyle that caused them to become ill in the first place.

People who want to bring about a change can do so by working with their doctor and a hypnotherapist to attack the cause of the problem rather than just treating the symptoms. The required changes in lifestyle are achieved more easily using hypnosis to reframe what the patient believes to be true. Patients can learn to like exercise and healthier food and to have a more positive outlook on the future.

Hypnosis is an effective tool that can also be used to improve sleep, stop smoking, reduce weight, and address anxiety, panic, or phobias. Recent information about placebos used in studies on medication for stress and anxiety has shown that in many cases the placebos were as effective as the medicine. More importantly, however, was the discovery that the change was not just mental—the belief that the patients were taking medication that would make them well actually caused physical changes to take place.

Given the power of prestigious suggestions in contributing to our health, it is important for medical professionals to be careful of the language they use and what they say to patients or to each other when patients are present.

In the end, Mom was right: you really *are* only as sick as you think you are.

twelve

"Trance-Formation" with Hypnosis

The Law of Control states that *you feel positive about yourself to the degree to which you feel you are in control of your own life.*

Health, happiness, and high performance begin with your taking complete control over your thinking, your actions, and your circumstances in the world around you.

People sometimes mistakenly think that the Law of Control means they can control all the events that befall them. I believe that once you accept responsibility for controlling your own life, you will find that things do seem to be more controllable. More important, though, is the fact that although you may not be able to control every event or person who enters your life, you can always control how you react or respond to them. Once you take control of choosing your own emotions, no one will be able to make you feel angry, guilty, or any other destructive negative emotion. Once you choose to react in a healthy, happy way, your life will instantly get better.

Having touched briefly on the history of hypnosis and some of its potential applications, I'll use this short chapter to review how hypnotic trances are used with proven action plans to bring about real change in the choices that clients make.

While the information on self-limiting beliefs is widely available, many people do not make the required changes in their beliefs in order to accept new material into their way of thinking. If nothing changes . . . nothing changes. Combining this new material with mental training has resulted in many interesting notes of thanks.

One of the most memorable experiences came as a result of offering a sales course to a telephone-directory sales team. After the program, the sales manager took me aside and said that a woman who worked for him was very bright, knew the material and the sales techniques, and seemed ambitious, but her sales were very low. He offered to pay for a private session if I would take the time to talk to her. In the session, we reviewed what we had talked about in the course and how she could see what we learned applying to her.

A week later, the sales manager called me, beginning the conversation with, "What have you done to Susan? She sold more this week than she has in the previous three months!" He went on to say that the most interesting thing was that he controlled the leads and gave them to the sales associates as they needed them. He said she had called in that morning to say she needed more leads and he had promised them to her by lunch. But he was busy and forgot about them until two in the afternoon, when she called back and said, "Are you going to give me those leads or what?" He said she had never been that forthright with him before, and he loved it. In the past, she would have patiently waited for him, but now she had become much more aggressive. He wanted me to have more sessions with his staff.

Six months later, I received a note from Susan saying how much her life had changed and how happy she was. Since our session, she had quit her job and followed her dream by returning to college and getting a degree. As much as I would like to take the credit for her blossoming, I only showed her where the door to a better future was and encouraged her to walk through it.

Napoleon Hill discovered years ago that we are what we think about and that if we can control what we think about, we can control who we are. There is considerable debate over how much of who we are comes about because we are hard-wired and cannot be controlled or changed easily and how much is a result of this core belief programming. The general consensus seems to lean further and further toward the programming side of the equation. A strong belief is growing that even a number of our physical characteristics are determined by our programming.

My mission is to assist people with the reprogramming of their mental computers, utilizing both personal and corporate venues. Personal venues include helping clients to control their weight, stop smoking, and establish personal goals. In the corporate environment, coaches and facilitators for the Canadian Hypnosis Institute work with business and sales organizations striving to build a more effective team.

We use powerful hypnotic suggestion techniques to provide improvement in a wide range of areas, including personal development, communication, motivation, sales, and teamwork. Programs include improving self-esteem and self-confidence and overcoming the fear of failure, the fear of success, the fear of prospecting, the impostor's syndrome, and several other issues that hold good people back. Clients in middle and upper management use hypnotic suggestions to reduce stress and set clearer corporate and personal goals. They complete powerful strategic plans and become more effective as leaders in selling the corporate vision.

As I've said, the use of the term *hypnosis* in the corporate world is somewhat uncommon, but the terms *visualization techniques* and *image practicing* are often used. Most methods of visualization, relaxation, imagination, meditation, and self-mind control—and even yoga and some martial arts—are or use basic hypnosis techniques. Although these methods utilize hypnosis, many training organizations tend to avoid the word *hypnotism* because either they are not staffed with trained hypnotherapists or they feel the idea of being hypnotized has a negative connotation in the boardroom. (I still believe in calling a rose a rose even though I know I may lose business from company executives who don't understand hypnosis or are hung up on an old belief that I may somehow take control of their minds.)

I trust that now that you have a basic understanding of hypnosis, what it really is, and how it works, you will use it to accomplish your goals and improve your life.

The next section focuses on helping you to identify and understand what those goals are—what it is you really want—and then showing you how to remove the limiting beliefs that are holding you back and preventing you from having already achieved them.

thirteen

The Biggest Obstacle

The Law of Choice states that *your life is the sum total of all of your choices up to this present time. Since you are always free to choose what you think about, you are in complete control of your life and everything that happens to you.*

The next part of the program is designed to bring you the best method of achieving the goals you truly desire and deserve regardless of what phase of life you are in. Studies conducted on adult learners prove that the best way for them to learn is through a multisensory method using interactive participation. This is particularly important in goal achievement. Just as you cannot learn to ride a bike by reading about it, you cannot achieve successful goals without becoming involved in the process. Or, as Aristotle said, "We must learn by doing the thing. For though you think you know it, you have no certainty until you try."

The single biggest obstacle to achieving goals successfully lies in our own self-limiting beliefs. Self-help and sales trainers teach people how to control their way of thinking by using affirmations, positive language, and positive self-talk, but many struggle with keeping the gatekeeper or negative voice from planting the seeds of self-doubt by invoking a limiting belief and undermining the whole process.

The old adage "We have met the enemy and he is us" is never truer than when we are goal setting. Our failure lies more often with our own thought process and the belief that we cannot succeed than with any outside obstacle. To overcome this internal self-defeating belief involves more than reading about it; it involves taking action. This book and the CD designed to go with it will provide you with the tools to do just that.

To accomplish participation in a non-classroom environment is not easy, but if you commit to utilizing the tools in this program and using the multisensory learning techniques, you will be on your way to success.

Success is dependent upon your participation and requires that you truly engage your thought process and complete the assignments. The CD uses hypnotic techniques to further involve the other senses in the learning process as well as remove limiting beliefs and empower the listener.

To get the most out of this program, follow the directions. You will find that as your thoughts change, so do your results.

I know these techniques are effective, as I have used them success-fully in a coaching program of ours in which participants met on a weekly basis to establish and achieve the goals they desire.

fourteen
Refuse to Set Goals

The Law of Expectations states that *whatever you expect with confidence tends to materialize in the world around you. You always act in a manner consistent with your expectations, and your expectations influence the attitudes and behaviors of the people around you.*

Remember, the messages we give our subconscious mind are carried out literally, so do you merely want to *set* goals, or do you want to *get* them? Effective goal *getting* is the key ingredient to success in any field. If you do not know where you are going, any road will take you there, but if you want to reach a specific destination, you stand a much better chance of doing so if you use a map.

Although I specialize mainly in corporate work, I am listed in the yellow pages as a hypno*therapist*, so I receive a lot of calls from people with a wide variety of issues. One area in which I have worked a lot is with people having various degrees of depression. The one thing that almost all of these people have in common is that they lack goals. They have trouble seeing a positive future and tend to think only about the things they don't want to happen to them. The commonality I have observed in the most optimistic and happy people I see is that they have goals and a clear vision of a positive future. It could be argued that the depression (cause) creates a lack of goals or a positive feeling for the future (effect). Or are the negative feelings for the future (cause) creating the depression (effect)?

The medical community tends to treat depression by raising the serotonin levels in the brain, which are normally lower in people suffering from depression. This same argument, when carried further, raises the question of whether the serotonin levels are lower because the person is depressed or whether the person is depressed because the serotonin levels are low.

It has been my experience that depression is often brought on when people cannot see a positive future or feel comfortable about the direction in which they are headed.

Myrna and I reached our financial goals early, sold our businesses, and moved south, where I spent my days puttering around the yard and fixing it up just the way I wanted it. Because I was not working or engaged in the community, I met few people, and as I completed the yard, I found it harder and harder to get up in the mornings. I did not feel as happy as I used to. My doctor diagnosed low levels of serotonin as the problem and said this was bringing on a state of mild depression. For a year, I took medication without real results. Then one day I realized that I had obtained most of my goals but had not established new ones. I decided that I had to get back to work, not for the money but for my own sanity. Myrna and I sat down and set a one- and five-year vision along with the goals we wanted to achieve along the way. Almost immediately I began to feel better. Suddenly I had something worth working toward. I began to join both professional and community volunteer groups. I decided to get rid of the medication, and within a short time, I had more energy and zest for life.

In discussing this with other people who have retired, I found many went through the same process. I know now that retiring is dangerous to your health unless you have a clear vision with firm goals as to what you want to accomplish during this phase of your life. I now know I will never retire completely. I will take more time for myself and I will do what I enjoy, but I will always have a vision and the corresponding goals to work toward. (One of my goals was to become an author, which resulted in my writing a weekly humor column, several business articles, and this book.)

I encourage you, for the sake of your health and well-being, to sit down and begin creating your future today.

Goal getting in its simplest form is simply laying out a map of where you want to go in your future. Maps are composed of the same three key elements you find when you arrive at the mall map and look for a particular store:

1. "You are here." You must know exactly where you are to begin with, which involves some self-inspection.

2. You must clearly understand where your desired destination is located. In the mall, you look at the directory for the specific store you want to go to and then find it on the map. People often claim to have set goals but find that their destinations are far too vague. Brian Tracy states that a goal should be so detailed and specific that you could send a child out to get it for you. The reason people tend to skip this step is fear. They are afraid that if they

commit to a specific goal that can be measured and don't achieve it, they have failed. If, on the other hand, they are not specific, making a goal such as, "In the future, I plan to be better off," then how can they fail? They have not said *when* in the future or defined exactly what "better off" means.

3. If you know where you are now and where you want to go, then navigating the most effective route becomes relatively simple.

To begin with, you must have an understanding of how the theories of goal getting and the universal mental laws affect the process.

The first key step will assist in establishing the specific starting point. You will be required to answer a number of questions, and I encourage you to take this part very seriously. A map is of little good if you do not know where you are starting from. Not only will this section assist you in determining clearly where you are, but it will also later reveal some of the roadblocks you have been putting in your way.

In the second key step, you will determine exactly where it is you want to go. Statements such as, "I want to have better health" or "I want more money" are not goals, because they do not mean anything. Is "more money" another dollar, another ten dollars, or a million dollars? Is money really the goal? Money is either just a way of keeping score in business or a vehicle that can offer you the opportunity for other desired results. Why do you want money? What are the results you are really looking for? By participating in these exercises, you will clearly define your goals, an important element in being able to achieve them. Only after you clearly define where it is you want to go on a map does the map become useful.

Finally, we will explore how using hypnosis will remove your roadblocks and make it easy to achieve your goals.

I trust you will use this program several times and will find the information rewards you as much as it has rewarded me over the past twenty years.

The self-hypnosis CD will alter your core belief system by removing the limiting beliefs holding you back. Follow the directions and you will experience incredible results.

Do not use the CD until you have worked through this entire book once. The workbook section includes some information you already know, but repeating the information will help your subconscious to take it as fact. Be patient and repeat the process often, and you will be amazed at your results. I know this will work for you because of all the e-mails, letters, and calls I have had from clients who have used this process successfully. In science, you know that a certain cause will always result in the same effect. The same principles hold true here. If it works for one person, it will work for all others.

The CD offers a full hypnosis session, which I recommend listening to every day for at least a week. Find a comfortable place where you can recline and remain comfortable without interruptions for the better part of an hour. Listening to the session just prior to falling asleep is effective, but participants are also encouraged to listen while sitting in a recliner or in some other place where they are able to complete the session without falling completely asleep every time they listen to it. This is a general hypnosis session to induce more self-confidence and power in the mind of the listener.

I recommend playing this track every day for the second week as well, and at least three times during week three. This track is also effective for reinforcement whenever the participant thinks it necessary.

The more intelligent and creative you are, the easier you will find it to enter a trance state, but only those with an IQ of less than 65 are impossible to hypnotize. If your determination and desire is strong enough, it is virtually impossible for you not to become hypnotized. The only thing that will prevent you from entering a hypnotic state is if after you read through the book, you still harbor fear or anxieties of letting yourself go. If you find this to be the case, we suggest that you re-read the earlier chapters on what hypnosis is and is not—and keep practicing. The more often you let yourself enter a state of trance, the easier and more effective it will become.

If at first you do not succeed, do not be discouraged. Repetition is a key element of hypnotic suggestion. The more often you engage in the process, the more effective the long-term results will be, so work your way through the book a number of times and listen to the CD as often as possible.

Often, it seems as though hypnosis is magic. You may find some instant results, but remember, this is not magic. You did not adopt the habits and beliefs you have now overnight, and they may not always disappear that quickly either. For the best long-term results, complete the entire program and reuse it again on a regular basis—and send me your success stories.

To begin, form and use affirmations daily, the least of which should include the following:

I am moving in the right direction . . .

Each day my goals are become clearer . . .

I am beginning to achieve more of the results I desire . . .

I love the direction my goals are taking me . . .

I can do this . . .

I have all the power and energy I need . . .

I choose to be happy . . .

I choose to be successful . . .

fifteen

Why Goals Must Be Written

The Law of Compensation states that *the universe is completely balanced and in perfect order. You will always be compensated in full for everything you do. You will get out what you put in. You can have more because you can contribute more.*

Every book has a different number of steps or ways of setting goals, but most agree on the following principles:

Steps to Goal Achievement

1. Decide what you want . . . and WRITE IT DOWN.

    a. Make it clear, specific, and detailed. (See it as completed.)

    b. Make it measurable and objective.

    c. Make it definite, make it ideal, and make it exciting. The more intense your burning desire—or the bigger the "why" you have—the stronger your motivation will be.

2. Set a deadline. Without a deadline, a goal is not a goal but merely a wish.

3. Identify the obstacles between you and your goal. What is holding you back?

4. Identify the knowledge and skills you will require to get from where you are to where you want to go. What one skill, if you had it and did it in an excellent fashion, consistently, over and over, would have the greatest positive impact on your life?

5. Identify the people, groups, and organizations whose help and cooperation will assist you in achieving your goals.

6. Create a detailed written plan and then identify the priorities.

7. Take action. Do something every day that moves you toward your goal or goals. Later in this book, you will read the story of a young man who, after hearing this while attending one of our seminars on the subject, quit his telemarketing job and moved to Los Angeles. His results were unbelievable.

8. Celebrate every step as a reminder that each small success is moving you in the right direction. Too many people focus only on the end result, such as being a hundred pounds lighter, and fail

to motivate themselves with a celebration each time they reach a milestone, be it losing ten pounds or one.

I am sure you will recognize these or similar steps from other goal-setting programs, but few ever explain the theory behind taking these steps or the best way to take them. Once you understand the theory, you will find it easier to design and stick with your own program.

In the following chapters, we will explore some of the theory behind the methods of goal getting we are using, as well as some key exercises to move you in the directions you desire. If this were a treadmill, you would not expect to increase your fitness by merely owning or looking at it. This is your book, and if you truly wish to make some changes, then work with it, fill in the blanks, re-read it . . . and celebrate. I cannot stress how important it is for you to celebrate and congratulate yourself at each step along the way.

The Law of Visualization states that *the world around you is an out-picturing of the world within you. The images you dwell upon affect your thoughts, feelings, and behavior. Whatever you visualize clearly and emotionally will eventually materialize in your world.*

We will learn how the power of visualization is put into play using hypnosis and how we can visualize more clearly if we first put our goals in writing. Authors and personal development gurus have written hundreds of great books on how to set or achieve goals. Most agree that for them to be real goals, you must write them down, but few explain why beyond the opening remarks. Once I understood the rationale for writing goals, the task became much easier and I achieved more of my goals.

As the owner of a corporate training company, I had the opportunity to hear and study a number of methods as well as meet and discuss several theories with the methods' authors. In assembling information for our own courses, we borrowed bits and pieces from several of these sources, putting the best of the best together. Over time, this resulted in the workbook section that is included for you to use. The program is very flexible, so you can tailor it to your own specific needs, making it very powerful as well.

You will recognize that many of the principles follow the universal laws. Wherever possible, we have also included the background of these concepts in order to explain why these principles are so important and effective, beginning with the one that states that all goals should be in writing.

I believe that Lou Tice of the Pacific Institute explained it to me better than any other author on the subject. Lou says in his teachings that millions of pieces of information bombard our minds every minute. Even as you sit here now, you are aware of reading the words on this page. At the same time, you are aware of how the paper feels, the size of the book, and the comfort of the chair you are sitting in. You are aware of other people who may be present, other objects in the room, the look of the lights, the sounds of the air conditioner and other noises in the room, as well as the sounds of traffic or noises from outside the room. The list of what is affecting your senses right now is almost endless. Despite all these distractions and your ability to be aware of them, if you focus, you are still able to put them aside and concentrate on the task at hand.

To keep our brains from overloading by trying to process all this information, we have developed mental filters known as the *reticular activating system*. This filtering system subconsciously analyzes all incoming information and then quickly decides whether the information is important to you or not. Only information considered important is processed, and the remainder is ignored by your mind.

For example, I recently bought a new four-door truck. I chose the new silver option because I hadn't seen many in that color. The next day, Myrna pulled up next to the truck in the parking lot of the hockey rink to talk to me and was surprised that it wasn't me but someone with a truck exactly like mine. Since then, I discovered there are four trucks on the same block as our office that are exactly the same as mine. I'm sure you have had a similar experience. I thought, where did all these identical vehicles come from? They weren't there last week. Of course, I knew that they were, it's just that I had now tuned my reticular activating system, and the silver trucks had become noticeable. Once you train your reticular activating system to see the opportunities you need to accomplish your goals, it will do so, and they will come much easier.

The easiest way to accomplish a goal is to program the filtering system to let in all of the information needed to realize it. For your subconscious mind to recognize what information is important, it must have as clear a picture of the goal as possible. To further engage the subconscious mind in opening a window for the information through the reticular activating system, it is important to repeat the new message while using as many of the senses as possible, remembering that the mind collects its information from all of our senses.

By writing down our goals, it introduces them to our subconscious mind in a number of ways. First, writing them down forces us to be more specific about them. The act of writing the goals also causes a sense of feeling, or a kinetic method of communicating with our subconscious mind. We see the words, stimulating our visual sense as we write them on the page. As we write, we say them in our mind, triggering our auditory sense. This becomes even more effective if we repeat the goals out loud. By imagining and writing the goals in the present tense, as though the goals have already been achieved, we can sense the "emotional feeling" of having accomplished them. This also aids in the visualization of the goals in our minds as we imagine what it would look like to have achieved them. If it is possible to experience the goal beforehand, such as happens when you test-drive the new car you may be buying or walk through the university you may be attending, it attaches an even stronger emotion to it. After she finished ninth grade, we sent our daughter Katherine to Youth University, a summer program where she lived in a residence hall and attended classes with other high school kids. She so fell in love with the idea of someday attending college that her marks moved from barely passing to honors, and she ended up getting a double degree because of the experience.

By simply thinking about our goals in our conscious mind, we may think we know what we want. Our subconscious mind will move us in the direction it feels best protects us. It develops these feelings based on how it has been programmed in the past. It is important, therefore, to reprogram the subconscious so that it readjusts the filtering system to allow through those things that assist in attaining the goals.

It takes more to achieve goals than just wishing it so in our conscious mind. This program includes the latest in this transformation technology, utilizing both the best in goal-setting techniques as well as using self-hypnosis to assist in reprogramming our thinking.

There is an age-old question to consider: do we believe what we see, or do we see what we believe? Our subconscious mind often only lets in the information it feels is relevant, based on what we already believe to be true or important, and because of this we may miss other opportunities. In class, I demonstrate it with the exercise that follows.

Holding this book with both hands outstretched, read the following paragraph. As you do, count the *F*s:

FINISHED FILES ARE THE RESULT OF YEARS OF SCIENTIFIC STUDY COMBINED WITH THE EXPERIENCE OF MANY YEARS OF EXPERTS.

The purpose of this exercise is to demonstrate how our mind works. If you have seen it before or if you took too long, you may have arrived at the right number, but go ahead and try it with a friend. You will find that having read through the paragraph, most people immediately see three *F*s. Some will see more on the first or second reading, but few will actually see all seven. Yet there they are. If your mind can be fooled into not seeing the *F*s, what else are you being fooled into not seeing?

This is one of the reasons we will spend so much time writing our goals out and carefully reviewing them a few times. Once you finish the exercises that follow, you will find you begin to see more of the *F*s in life.

sixteen

Why Goals Must Be Positive

The Law of Cause and Effect states that *everything happens for a reason. For every cause, there is an effect, and for every effect, whether you know it or not, there is a specific cause or causes. There are no accidents. You can achieve anything you want in life. All you have to do is first decide exactly what it is you want, determine what others have done to achieve those same results, and then do the same things they did.*

We know from the study of behavior that specific actions will create the results we experience. In fact, there is an old adage that insanity is doing the same thing over and over but expecting different results.

We discussed earlier how people tend to act in a predictable way depending on the beliefs they hold about themselves and others. If all results are the product of an action and if the action is a response to core beliefs, then changing the things we believe will cause us to act differently, thereby producing a different result. By studying the relationship between core beliefs and actions, we can then determine what results to expect based on the beliefs a person holds.

Knowing that the same actions will produce the same results, we are able to achieve goals by simply imitating the beliefs of someone else who has obtained the same goals we want to achieve.

The subconscious mind is not logical—it holds our beliefs without question and carries out orders or directives given to it. The subconscious is unable to tell the difference between what is real and what is not. By stating a goal in the present tense, your mind will feel what it is like to have already achieved it and will begin to act accordingly. That is to say, by thinking you are successful already in any area, your mind will cause you to act in the same manner that other successful people do, and those actions will bring about the success you desire.

In addition to this, every time your mind fires off an electrical impulse carrying a message to your body, commanding it to do something, it builds a neuron highway in the brain. The same impulse is fired whether the body is actually doing the action or just imagining the action. The more often this same message is fired, the better the highway we build. That is why practice doesn't make perfect and only perfect practice makes perfect.

Remember that perfect practice is created in sports by using visualization techniques to build these highways and improve performance. When the great Jack Nicklaus said, "Every shot I make, I make first in my mind," he was setting up his mind to believe he had already achieved it. Believing your goals can be achieved will cause you to act in accordance with those beliefs, and the accomplishment of the goals will result.

For this reason, when you begin to write your goals, it is very important to be as specific as possible, engage as much emotion as possible, and state the goal as though it has already been accomplished.

The Law of Affirmation states that *fully 95 percent of your thinking and feeling is determined by the way you talk to yourself. Your inner dialogue is accepted as commands by your subconscious mind. Talk to yourself positively and constructively all the time, even when you don't feel like it.*

Affirmations are the self-talk or personal statements we use when speaking to ourselves. Affirmations are highly recommended for effectively achieving goals. Again, these statements describe the goal we wish to achieve in the present tense and using the first person. The third element is to make the statements using positive language.

When we say positive language, we mean in terms of concrete rather than abstract, not in the sense of good rather than bad. The reason for this is the subconscious mind thinks in pictures and emotions, so it is vital to form all communication with the subconscious using positive imagery, as there are no negative pictures.

For example, if I tell you to close your eyes, take a deep breath, and not think of the Eiffel Tower, what image goes immediately through your mind? If you are normal, it will be an image of the Eiffel Tower, because there are no pictures of the negative *don't*. The only way to prevent your thinking of the Eiffel Tower is to immediately substitute the image by thinking of something else, such as the Taj Mahal.

That is why it is so important to state what you want, not what you do not want. Avoid making statements such as, "I don't waste time," as there is no picture of "don't waste time." A positive picture would be, "I plan each day the first thing in the morning, so I can accomplish more."

A statement attached to a powerful emotion will be more effective in achieving the goal. See yourself accomplishing the goal, and let yourself feel the emotion attached to its successful accomplishment. Form pictures in your mind that include how those accomplishments will affect those around you.

I cannot stress too much how important language is when communicating with the subconscious mind. Our mind does differentiate between the words, and it guides us in exactly the direction we have stated. It is better to *get* goals than just to *set* goals. So when you think of your goals, do not think about things you are setting out (hoping) to achieve, but think and talk only about getting or achieving those things. As mentioned already, some people fear using positive statements because they believe that if they state they are going to do something and then they do not do it, others—or, worse, themselves—will see them as having failed. That is why the word "try" is used so much: "I will *try* to make more money this year." By setting this as a goal, I have already built in a safety valve and sought permission to fail by using the word "try." At the end of the year, if I have not succeeded, I do not have to be accountable to it, because I only said I would try, not that I would definitely do it. Remember, though, that you only fail once you have stopped working toward your goal. You can fall down numerous times on the road of life, but you only fail once you refuse to get back up. Had I made the goal specific but not reached it, I am almost sure I would be in a position to say, "I may not have made the goal, but look at how much better I did than last year. I am moving in the right direction." Then I would celebrate and begin planning my next year.

Sales courses often have salespeople write out affirmations on index cards and tape them to their mirrors at home. It is then suggested that every morning when they look in the mirror they repeat the affirmation.

The theory is that if we repeat something to ourselves often enough, eventually it will become a belief, and once we believe it to be true, it will affect our actions, causing us to achieve the results we want. (This is one of the secret reasons I have repeated myself in this book so often.)

An affirmation for a salesperson, then, might be something like, "I am a successful salesperson." This affirmation is in the right format, in that it includes the present tense, the first person, and a positive image. The problem some of us have—and I say "us" because I assume if I have a problem then the whole world has a similar problem—is the little gatekeeper who sits on our shoulder and whispers in our ear. His or her job is to protect us by making sure that everything we tell ourselves is the truth, at least as we perceive the truth to be. So, as we repeat the statement, "I am a successful salesperson," the little voice will say things like, "What about the deal you lost yesterday?" or "Why are you over-drawn at the bank?" or some other self-defeating truth that would take the power out of the affirmation.

This is where the true power of hypnosis comes into play, because if anything is asleep during the hypnosis process, it is this gatekeeper. We will review later how to form a good hypnotic suggestion, which is really just a good affirmation given to someone in a hypnotic state.

seventeen

Specific Goals Yield Specific Results

The Law of Clarity states that *the clearer you are about what you want and what you are willing to do to get it, the more likely it is that you will* be lucky and get what you want.

Clarity of desired goals is a magnet that draws good luck to you.

It is crucial to make all of your goals as specific as possible. Many people claim to have a goal of obtaining more money. Personal-development guru Anthony Robbins says that when someone tells him this at a seminar, he reaches into his pocket and digs out a couple of coins and gives them to that person. This is more money than they had, so they should be happy. They are not happy, however, because that is not what they meant. He tells them to be more specific.

Remember, the subconscious mind does not do any critical thinking. It takes things literally, so in order for the subconscious to know what you mean, you must be specific. If having more money is one of your goals, state exactly how much more money you want. If you wish to lose weight, state how many pounds exactly. We protect ourselves from accountability by purposely being vague when setting goals so that we never have to admit failure. The problem is, our subconscious mind requires clear direction so that it can let in the right information to achieve the desired outcome. It is therefore imperative to be as specific as possible. Do not let fear hold you back.

Once you have made your goals as specific and real as possible in your mind, get out of the way. This is not to say that you sit back and wait. You still have to create the opportunity through further education and putting yourself in the right place and around the right people.

What I mean by that statement is that you should not limit yourself to exact details or options for achieving the goal, but rather create opportunities and then leave yourself open for the goal to come in any way that it may. Become ready to seize unexpected opportunities.

Some companies teach goal setting in a logical method, and for some number-type goals it works. For example, a company that keeps good statistics, like the insurance industry, might have its people set goals in the following manner. (All numbers have been made up to make the math easier, as it is the principles that we wish to explore here). It may suggest that if an agent wishes to set a goal to earn $100,000 next year, all he or she has to do is follow a formula. For example, if an average selling commission on a sale was $1,000, the goal setter would have to make one hundred sales per year, or two per week for fifty weeks of the year. In order to make two sales per week, if the industry average required two appointments per sale, then the salesperson would have to make four appointments each week to generate the sales. Statistically, the experience of the company might have been that in order to make an appointment, three quick presentations were required. If so, every week, twelve presentations would have to be made to get the four appointments. If the average number of appointments booked to get one presentation were two—because statistically one will cancel—then to reach the goal of twelve presentations, twenty-four presentations would have to be booked.

Again, if the statistics show that to get a presentation, five people have to be asked, then to get the twenty-four appointments, one hundred and twenty people have to be asked. If the planned workweek is five days, then the logical first order of business every day should be to call twenty-four people.

If these statistics were accurate, an average salesperson following the training and adhering to the plan of simply calling twenty-four people every day will make $100,000. The process is that simple: just make the twenty-four calls every day (cause) and the sales (effect) will follow. The problem is that our subconscious mind is not logical. Many goals cannot be defined logically in numbers, so they have to be put into a form the subconscious mind communicates in or understands, and that form is emotions, pictures, or information given through the other senses. That is not to say these goals are not as specific as earning $100,000 a year, just that they may not be as logical.

I have stated before that the subconscious mind does not know the difference between what is real and what is not. If a goal is made to seem real enough, the subconscious mind will accept it as true and move to make it so. The best method of creating a goal is to make it as real as possible in the right side of the brain and then get out of the way and let the subconscious mind begin moving toward achieving it.

You will be amazed how often a goal is achieved through an avenue that you had not planned for. Too often, we use rational, logical thinking and get in our own way of achieving our goals. Let me give you an example from my own life.

You will recall from my history that some years ago I experienced a personal financial correction. Politically speaking, you would say that my status was realigned, my position re-engineered. I became financially challenged, as both my company and my personal positions were downsized from that of being very well off to that of a pauper. Political correctness aside, what I'm trying to say is, I went broke.

Like others in oil-rich areas, our company relied on and invested heavily in the oil industry, and when the government suddenly changed the rules, the oil companies left our community. I did not have a positive vision of the future, so when the economy crashed, so did I. With one credit card left, I was now free to start over. I was free to do whatever I wanted, but I did not see it that way.

I was devastated. Of course, in hindsight I realize that had I not endured that experience, I would never have discovered my real treasure. It was because of those difficulties that I met Myrna, whom I later married, and now, with her, I have two great sons, Carson and Liam. Although the financial collapse resulted in my first wife leaving me and moving away, it brought me to the realization that I had better take a stronger interest in the two daughters we had together. Even though we ended up living miles apart, our relationship grew stronger because of the new importance I placed on it.

Myrna believed in personal power as well as the power of positive thinking. Not only did she believe in the power of the subconscious mind, she taught others how to use it in courses she presented to real-estate boards in several cities. She held the astonishing belief that things would work out for the better, and they always seemed to. Leading by example, she helped me overcome my budding self-doubt, and together we started a real-estate company on a credit card and a shoestring. (I do not necessarily suggest that you try this at home.)

Myrna suggested we set both short- and long-term goals. "Plan for things and they will materialize," she would tell me. My belief had turned negative because of this experience, and although I had a great deal of doubt, I agreed to play along.

The financial collapse had forced me to sell my airplanes. I really missed being able to fly, and it hurt my ego to be grounded, so one of my desires was to own another airplane. I could not write it down as a short-term goal, however, because it was unreasonable to think I could own one given my current position. My rational, logically thinking conscious mind told me this was an unrealistic goal for someone who did not know where next week's groceries were going to come from, but with Myrna's encouragement, I wrote it down.

Within a couple of weeks of setting this goal, a doctor who had flown with me on a number of occasions called to say he missed my airplane as well, and he suggested we become partners in a new one. He said he wanted to buy an airplane even though he did not have a pilot's license and knew little about aircraft. If I would agree to be his partner and the pilot, he said that he would buy the aircraft and that I could pay him for my half when I could afford it.

I was startled by how quickly this goal seemed to materialize out of nowhere, but I declined the offer. I just could not imagine ever being able to pay him back, and I felt as though he was offering me charity, which further bruised my ego.

A week later, he called again to say he had found a Cherokee 6. "It's exactly like your old one, and I'm going to buy it," he told me. Then he added, "I don't have a pilot's licence, and I don't know anything about airplanes. If you don't help me by becoming my partner, it will be your fault if I end up making a bad deal."

It was hard to refute that kind of twisted logic; besides, guilt is a powerful tool. The deal was completed, and what I had thought was an unrealistic goal was achieved within weeks of setting it. If I had tried to set this goal logically, it would not have happened, as I would have realized how impossible it was to achieve it in the normal or logical process of goal setting.

That is not the end of the story. Myrna and I, still flat broke, flew this airplane to Red Deer to attend a real-estate sales rally just a few weeks later. The speaker's flight had been delayed, and he would not arrive in Calgary until late. The organizer knew we had an aircraft and asked if we would mind meeting his flight and bringing Mark, the speaker, back to Red Deer to save time. As both Myrna and I were interested in speaking and training as a career, we were happy to get an opportunity to visit privately with Mark during the flight.

On the flight back to Red Deer, Mark told us that he too had just gone through a financial crisis. He shared his belief system with us, which included the theory that we should all live at the level we desire, and the money will follow. He went on to explain that his most expensive asset was his thousand-dollar suit, because looking the part and feeling the part of being successful was important. He said that in his mind, he was already rich; he just didn't have the cash yet. I found it strange that he was making a living telling people—many of whom were far better off financially than he was—how to become more successful. It seemed ironic that he was living as though he had already realized his goals when he hadn't yet.

After his talk, he convinced us to buy his new self-published book, *Future Diary*, which was a guide on how to write your goals as though they had already been achieved. Interesting, I thought to myself, and gave it to Myrna, who filled out the spaces on the flight home before filing the book away.

We had an opportunity to meet Mark again a number of times over the next few years. Then, in the early 1990s, a local businessperson brought him to speak in our city. Later, we all went out for supper, and Myrna brought her copy of the book, which she confessed she had not looked at for several years. To her amazement, we had achieved almost every goal she had written in it. What really surprised her was a picture she had drawn of what she thought the perfect house would look like. Although I had not seen the drawing, I had just finished designing and building us a house that looked surprisingly like the picture she had drawn, complete with triangular windows. Mark was very interested in the story, and he offered us copies of his newest book. He told us his goal was to have it become a best seller and then write forty sequels to it. He even shared some of the corny titles. I remember my skeptical side thinking he would be lucky if he ever had one become a best seller, but I kept my thoughts to myself and admired the confidence he had in his vision.

A couple of months later, I heard a woman talking to our reception-ist at the front desk. I could hear her saying she was the new manager of a local radio station, and I found it intriguing that she "had" to meet Myrna. When the receptionist showed this woman into our common office, she began shaking Myrna's hand and said she had to know how Myrna had become so well connected.

The woman then told us how she had just returned from attending a course in New York City and said the speaker had floored her when he began talking about goal setting. He started by saying he had a friend, Myrna Park, who had successfully used his techniques, and he then relayed the story about the house. She finished by saying she could not believe that she had paid a lot of money to travel all the way to the Big Apple to hear a speaker who then talked about someone who worked just blocks away from her station. "Not only that," she finally added, "he told us about his new book, which is taking off and is going to be a world best seller. He called it *Chicken Soup for the Soul!*"

The book *Future Diary*, by Mark Victor Hansen, which we had used so effectively, demonstrated the power of projecting oneself into the future when writing goals. Stating goals as though they have already been achieved makes them easier to visualize specifically and is a widely accepted technique simply because it has been proven to work.

eighteen

Your Belief System
and Your Goals

The Law of Substitution states that *your conscious mind can hold only one thought at a time, positive or negative. You can decide to be happy by substituting positive thoughts for negative ones. Your mind is like a garden. Either weeds or flowers will grow.*

As part of the process of establishing where you are now, you must identify what self-limiting beliefs are holding you back in order to be able to remove them. This is one reason for setting your goals as though you have already accomplished them. By seeing yourself as having obtained the goal, your subconscious mind has an opportunity to make the mental adjustments you will need to make to comfortably handle the goal.

In the case of wanting more money, Brian Tracy explains that if you suddenly get a million dollars, you had better learn quickly how to become a millionaire or you will soon lose it. That is to say, you have to make a mental switch before receiving the goal, or you will not be able to handle it.

For example, I worked with a client named Larry, who had reached a net worth of a million dollars several times only to lose much of it each time he passed that milestone. He did not consciously set out to lose the money and was very disappointed, even becoming depressed when he did lose it, so why did it keep happening?

During hypnotherapy sessions, Larry revealed that he believed money was not that important. When he was young, he heard many times that rich people are not happy and that most obtained their wealth by walking over other people or by being dishonest. Larry remembered hearing other suggestions, such as, "It's better to be happy than rich," like it was a choice and he could not have both.

The mark of being wealthy or rich in Larry's mind was to have his net worth exceed a million dollars. When his net worth did pass this milestone, he subconsciously felt he was now becoming one of those rich people.

We are motivated either by fear or desire, and the strongest emotion always wins out over the weakest. Like most of us, Larry had the desire to make a great deal of money. However, Larry's strongest emotion was the fear of rejection and of becoming an unhappy, greedy, dishonest, and disliked rich person. He had a strong desire to be loved, liked, respected, and happy. Becoming a millionaire, as it was defined in his mind, came into conflict with his stronger emotional goals. To move him toward his desire and away from his fears, Larry's subconscious mind would take steps by removing the obstacle: the million dollars.

Once Larry understood the problem and reprogrammed his subconscious mind to understand that he could have both the money and his other personal goals, he was able to break through that million-dollar barrier and go on to accumulate greater wealth.

I have told this story a number of times at seminars, and someone usually says, "Boy, just let me deal with that problem. I would have no problem hanging on to the money." Most of us think we are different. Just give us a chance and we will not feel uncomfortable or lose the money.

Then recently, after addressing a group of professional salespeople, I had just finished relaying this story when Fred, a fellow sitting at the front, said, "That happened to me."

"What happened?" I asked.

"I won over a million dollars in 1984, and within two years I had lost it all," Fred replied, and several of his coworkers laughed at him, saying things like, "Sure you did."

"Really," Fred said. Then, turning to his boss, he added, "You tell them."

His boss looked around the table and asked Fred if he was sure he should. Fred confirmed it was okay, and his boss told how he had known Fred at that time and how Fred had indeed won that much money and then lost it all.

The rest of the group was now quiet, interested in knowing how that could have happened. Fred told them he did not really know why, but he felt guilty about having such good luck when most of his friends were struggling. He was uncomfortable around his friends, and it seemed to be understood that when they went out for meals, drinks, or parties, he should buy. Why wouldn't he? Didn't he have all the money? He said he lent others money that never was repaid, he invested in their hare-brained schemes that were doomed to failure, and he bought new cars, new homes, and whatever else he fancied. Then he said, "One day I woke up and the money was all gone. I had to sell the house and cars to pay the bills, and I was broke."

In a similar study, a group of lower-income people who had become instant millionaires were tracked alongside a second group of people who had grown up in affluence but had become bankrupt. Over a ten-year period, the study found that a high percentage of the instant millionaires had lost most of their new wealth, while during the same time period the formerly wealthy people became wealthy once again.

It is as though we have an internal thermostat that is similar to the one regulating the heat in your home. If the temperature becomes lower than the setting, the furnace kicks in and heats the house up to the set temperature. If the heat in the house becomes higher than the setting, then the furnace stops or the air conditioning turns on until the temperature is brought back down to the setting. To move to and remain at a different economic level, you must learn to reset your internal thermostat. The easiest way to do that is to visualize yourself already being there. See who your friends would be, what you would be doing differently, what you would own, how you would invest. The clearer and more detailed the picture, the more comfortable you will become with it. As you become more comfortable with this picture, your subconscious mind begins to readjust the setting of where it believes you should be.

It is important to understand your beliefs and how they affect your goals. It is important to know what your goals are specifically and how they harmonize with each other. Picture yourself living in balance after successfully having achieved all of your desires.

Do you have some negative programming that you have to deal with at a subconscious level? Remember, the subconscious mind is not logical or rational. You may understand your goals from a conscious point of view, such as Larry did, but think about what your core beliefs are. Do they determine how successful you will be?

To help you achieve your goals and reprogram the beliefs that may be holding you back, take a minute to note some of the core beliefs you hold that may be in conflict with your goals. List some of the beliefs that may be holding you back. If you have trouble with this part, discuss it with your coach or hypnotherapist.

nineteen

Beliefs Determine Action, and Action Produces Results

We have discussed how we tend to act in accordance with what we believe and how the way we act brings about the results we get. If you are not happy with the results you are currently getting, the best way to change them is to change your current beliefs.

The last chapter explained how if you suddenly receive a million dollars and want to keep it, you must learn to become a millionaire. You must develop a millionaire mind, believing that you can be who you want to be and still have a million dollars. One way to learn how to be a millionaire is to set the goal as though you have already achieved it. Experience it first in your mind and learn the feeling of having the money. By the way, do not run out and begin buying yourself expensive items, as that is not what most millionaires do. If this is your idea of what a millionaire is, then your first assignment is to read the book *The Millionaire Next Door*, by Thomas J. Stanley and William D. Danko.

In the mid to late 1970s, the oil industry was going wild, and the small city of Grande Prairie, Alberta, claimed to have one of the highest numbers of millionaires per capita in Canada. Many of the local young businesspeople were on top of the world. They had invested heavily into oil-dependent ventures, and they had become wealthy. Then, in 1980, the government introduced a new National Energy Program. Within months, the resource industry crashed, real estate prices were cut in half, oil companies moved to the U.S., local businesses closed, and hundreds of people claimed bankruptcy. Many of these people started over again, knowing that they had worked their way to the top before and believing in their minds that they could do it again. Many of these same people made more money faster in the slower economy that followed than they had the first time around. Their reticular activating system was tuned in, and when they saw new opportunities, they seized them. Many of these same people are now the wealthiest business leaders in the community. This reinforces the belief that once our comfort zone—or mind—has been stretched, it never shrinks back to its original size. The people who were successful once are often successful again, because they know it is possible. This may also be the reason the average millionaire goes through two or three bankruptcies before he is ready to hold on to his new fortune.

As your reticular activating system lets in the information that is important to obtaining your goals, you will begin to see opportunities. Opportunities have always been there, but they were previously overlooked or filtered out by the subconscious mind. The writing down of goals opens up a window in the reticular activating system, and suddenly the opportunities become obvious.

To understand this better, remember the truck story from earlier. Often, we like a vehicle because it is a little unusual, maybe a rare model, a new color, or a special edition. What happens to you after you take the new car home? Within days, you see the same vehicle everywhere. They are all over the place, but why had you never seen them before? Suddenly, these vehicles are important to you, and your subconscious mind reprograms the reticular activating system to bring anything that it sees regarding these vehicles to your attention. You can be driving down the street at fifty miles an hour while passing a parking lot, and you will still notice a car like yours out of the corner of your eye.

How does changing your reticular activating system assist you with goal setting? Do you remember a time when you were at a party or some other place where a number of people were talking? While you were talking at one side of the room, someone on the other side of the room uttered the most important words in the world to your subconscious mind: your name. It was as though your name cut through all the other noise, like a knife coming straight to your ear. Someone said your name, and although you were not even aware of the other conversation taking place, you suddenly turned to see who was talking about you. We have programmed our name to come straight through our filtering systems, and it does.

Other words important to your goals will come through as well. If you are a Realtor at the same party and your goal is to list or sell houses, and if you have done a good job of programming your subconscious mind, then the following words spoken across the room will cut through as well: "transfer," "move," "list," "expand," "downsizing." These and several other words that are important to real estate will cause a Realtor's head to turn to see who said them.

If one of your goals is to run a marathon, you will begin noticing articles and magazines everywhere telling you how to train. You will see sales that offer the right shoes and will notice posters for training runs or local races. You will hear others talking about running and be drawn into their conversations. You will see running tracks or paths, and you will notice what other runners are wearing. I know, because I do not notice any of these things, but as we drive through new cities, Myrna, the family runner, sees them all.

This filtering system is a very powerful tool, and that is why it is important to program it by writing your goals clearly and specifically. Once the new goals have been firmly set into your subconscious mind, your filters are readjusted. Suddenly, you see everything that will help you move toward the obtainment of those goals.

That is why only "when the student is ready, the teacher will appear." The teacher, always there, remained unseen until the student was ready. Plant the seeds to your goals deep in the subconscious and the opportunities to achieve them will begin appearing everywhere.

The belief must be supported with a healthy dose of persistence.

The Law of Persistence states that *if you persist long enough in the pursuit of wealth, you must inevitably succeed. Obstacles are stepping stones to success, as long as you learn from every setback and disappointment.*

Persistence
Nothing in the world can take the place of persistence.
  Talent will not; nothing is more common than unsuccessful men with talent.
  Genius will not; unrewarded genius is almost a proverb.
  Education will not; the world is full of educated derelicts.
  Persistence and determination alone are omnipotent.
—Calvin Coolidge, thirtieth President of the United States

I believe Coolidge was close, but not entirely right. I have met some very persistent yet not successful people. If you want to meet a few, attend a meeting for one of the multilevel marketing companies operating in your area. Not that there is anything wrong with multilevel marketing, but ask the producers what their biggest challenge is, and they will tell you it is finding other good producers to recruit as sellers. Many of the people they find are very persistent, almost to the point of being obnoxious or zealous in their belief of the opportunity given to them, yet they are still unable to produce. In time, this zealousness dissipates, and they wander off to find an even better opportunity to represent.

So, if not persistence, then what is left? Belief! Only by truly believing that the goal is possible and that you deserve to achieve the goal can it be finally realized. Many persistent people hide their lack of confidence or belief in the goal. They may even believe that they are not worthy of the goal, which they hide in their zealous persistence of it.

The real key to your goals is the unwavering belief that you can achieve them.

twenty

WARNING: This Book Will Change Your Life!

The Law of Habit states that *95 percent of everything you do is the result of your habits, either helpful or hurtful.*

You can develop habits of success by practicing and repeating success behaviors repeatedly until they become automatic.

Take this program seriously. Invest some time in it. Be honest about what you really want in life, and these pages will transform your future. Clients report that this exercise excited them, because for the first time they knew exactly what they wanted.

Some people have changed careers or set new financial objectives. Others have moved or made other life-altering commitments after establishing clearly what they wanted and how to achieve it.

An employer sent a group of employees to one of our goal-setting sessions, including a large young man with a very long ponytail. This fellow worked as a telemarketer, and it was obvious he had not wanted to attend. The young man sprawled all over his desk, looking completely bored and disinterested in the program. Suddenly, something Myrna or I said clicked inside, and he began taking notes.

The boss called us within a few days to say when they returned home, the young man quit his job to follow his dream. I began to apologize, as our intent is not to have clients lose employees, but the boss laughed and said he was excited for the young man. It seems he wanted to write articles and design websites for heavy metal bands, and he knew that would not happen if he stayed in his small town, so he moved to California. The boss said it was as though suddenly a fire had been lit under him.

Within a month, the boss reported that the young man had landed a job writing for a heavy metal magazine and was designing websites on the side. Then, a year later, the boss told us the young man had called him to say that a band in England had hired him to design a website and then flew him to England to be with them when they launched it to begin their world tour. His former employer was excited as he told us how this young man had realized his dream by simply setting the goal.

Most clients make some changes. They spend more quality time with their loved ones, start a savings program, take better care of their health, or go back to school. Some set new priorities and others turn troubled businesses or marriages around.

Once you unleash the power of your subconscious mind and give it clear instructions as to what you really want, it will find a way to get it! The human mind is incredibly powerful.

Many people spend a lifetime wandering through their life in a state of confusion. We all want so many different things that we never decide to really go after or achieve any of them.

The simple exercises in this book will assist you in making the changes you truly desire. Redo the pages as often as you like, follow the directions, be honest, and you will be amazed at what you will achieve.

Finally, send me your success stories so we can use them in our next program to help others.

Take your time. *Do not* fill in all the questions right now, but rather spend some time thinking about the answers. This is not a race, and you will benefit more if you take your time. Give your mind time to digest the material: go for a walk or sleep on the questions. Keep the book handy, but do not feel you have to complete all of the exercises right away. You will find the answers beginning to materialize clearly in your mind.

Find a quiet space where you can take the time to form your answers when you are relaxed. Keep the book in a place where you will read it again after you have had time to think about both the questions and your answers. Change, delete, or add new items until you have written exactly what you want.

Set the book aside for a month and then do all of the exercises again. Like a navigator, you will reach your destination by reviewing your goals and rechecking your position. Then, you will continue on course by adjusting and making the corrections as needed.

This tool is for your benefit. Sometimes it may take hours, days, or even months to describe in detail the life you really want, while at other times it may take only a few minutes to jot down your first ideas. Use the exercises in whatever way will serve you best.

The objective of these exercises is to:

1. Decide exactly what it is you really want and then write it down.
2. Create your own personal blueprint to achieve the goals you want.
3. Set deadlines for each phase of each goal.
4. Determine what knowledge and skills you will need to achieve your goals.
5. Identify the critical people and resources you will need to accomplish your goals.
6. Determine what limiting beliefs may be holding you back and remove them so that your goals become your reality.

twenty-one

If Success Were Inside Your Comfort Zone, You Would Already Be Successful

The Law of Purpose states that *definitiveness of purpose is the starting point of all wealth. To become wealthy, you must decide exactly what you want, write it down, and then make a plan for its accomplishment. Successful people "think on paper."*

This exercise is just to get you thinking. List four successful goal-getting experiences you have had (for example, going to college, buying your first new home, or finding your current career or business) and how you felt when you accomplished them.

1. _____

_____

2. _____

_____

3. _____

_____

4. _____

_____

If you could do anything right now—and money, time, commitments, and responsibilities were not an issue—what would the top four things be? Be creative and just write down the things that come first to your mind. Don't analyze whether they are realistic or not.

1. _____

_____

2. _____

_____

3. _____

_____

4. _____

_____

If you knew that you could not fail, what five things would you do?

1. _____

_____

2. _____

_____

3. _____

_____

4. _____

_____

5. _____

_____

What are you afraid of? What is stopping you from already having achieved these goals? Write the first thoughts that come to your mind.

1. _____

_____

2. _____

_____

3. _____

_____

4. _____

_____

What usually stops us is the fear of leaving our comfort zone. The first experience we have in doing anything contains the most fear. The more we do it and succeed, the more we stretch our comfort zone and the easier it becomes. Eventually, we wonder how we could have ever been so silly. There was a time when I had so much fear of public speaking that I could not speak in front of even a few friends. Now I don't believe there is an audience large enough that could cause that fear to return. I love speaking, and the bigger the group, the more adrenaline I have. My inner voice used to say that I would make mistakes and embarrass myself. Now I know that I *will* make mistakes when I speak, but it will only endear audiences to me and cause them to bond with me. The mistakes give me the opportunity to comment on my making them and to make my audience laugh—not at me, but with me.

The key is to ask yourself, "What is the worst possible thing that could happen to me?" Then, reframe the question so it can work to your advantage. Ask yourself this question: "What is the worst thing that can happen if I don't go for it?"

I have an older retired friend who had a very successful career and now spends a lot of time volunteering for a junior football team. I discovered he had been the captain of a junior team when he was a kid, and when he became too old to play, they made a team trophy out of his helmet. Fifty years later, it is still awarded to the team's most valuable player. Several teams offered him opportunities to play professionally, but it was during a time when pro players were not that well paid.

This fellow's father did not want him to play and offered him a new car if he would turn the offers down and go into the family business. I don't know the reasons why he decided not to accept the offers—perhaps it was fear of disappointing his father, or maybe it was the fear of going pro, or maybe the desire to remain safely in his own community. It doesn't matter now what the reason was, but I know, from listening to him talk about that opportunity and about some of his teammates who became football heroes of the day, that he paid a far bigger price in not pursuing his dreams than he would have paid had he gone for it.

Don't let anything hold you back, whatever your reason is. In time, it will not seem to have been a good one. Don't sell your dreams short. If you can see them clearly in your mind, they are possible.

Practice visualization techniques or use self-hypnosis so you can see yourself achieving your goals from a safe place. The more you visualize or see yourself succeeding, the more your comfort zone stretches.

The five good reasons your inner voice will use to persuade you not to continue doing these assignments are as follows:

1. **Fear:** Fear stands between you and your dreams, armed with "what-ifs." What if I look foolish? What if I make a mistake? What if I fail? Fear will cause you to imagine the worst possible failures, cooling your desires.

2. **Self-doubt:** Self-doubt is the result of fear amplifying the weaker parts of your skills or talents. You end up creating all the reasons why your skills or talents will prevent you from succeeding until you believe that you have no talent at all. Even when you know you should proceed, self-doubt creates an inner paralysis.

3. **Numbness:** Numbness occurs when stress leaves you wondering what it is you really want. In this state, people may know they are unhappy, but they have no idea why.

4. **Self-limiting beliefs:** Classifying yourself or others can limit your dreams. Don't buy into general limiting beliefs about your age, gender, religion, ethnicity, or economic background. There are numerous examples of similar people who have more limited resources or talents than you do who have defied these limiting beliefs and become extremely successful. Only you are responsible for your success, and only you can stand in your way.

5. **Procrastination:** There are always good reasons to put off making changes in your life: not enough time, not enough money, the moon is in the wrong house, and so on. However, there comes a point at which you either take charge and change or let the excuses become permanent. We tend to justify our procrastination by telling ourselves we are just being cautious.

Make this the time you are going to ignore all these good reasons and forge ahead. Begin with truly working on this initial plan to decide what you want and how you will get out of your way.

twenty-two

Understanding Your Goals and You

The Law of Expression states that *whatever is expressed is impressed.* *Whatever you say to yourself with emotion generates thoughts, ideas, and behaviors consistent with those words. Be sure to talk about the things you want, and refuse to talk about the things you don't want.*

Happiness is the progressive realization of a worthy goal or ideal. The opposite of happiness is depression, which is the *lack* of a worthy goal or ideal.

Goals give you a feeling of power and purpose in life.

Goals release energy and trigger new ideas for goal attainment.

Goals build persistence, drive, and determination, and when you have clear goals, every failure is a learning experience that brings you closer to success.

If Goals Are That Powerful, Why Don't More People Set Them?

1. The importance of goals is not normally taught in school, and few people ever learn anything about them.

2. Do you remember learning how to set goals? Most people do not know how to set goals, yet the most successful people, companies, and countries set goals.

3. Fear of rejection. Some people are afraid that others will laugh at them if they set a goal and do not reach it. We suggest that you keep your goals confidential and only share them with like-minded people who will support you in their attainment. Those closest to you will often want to protect you from being hurt, so they will explain why you should not set goals that are too ambitious. Others will fear that you may actually achieve them, leaving them behind, so rather than set higher goals themselves, they find it easier to bring yours down.

A study carried out in 1953 showed that only 3 percent of a graduating class at Yale University had written goals. After twenty years, a follow-up study revealed that those 3 percent had a net worth more than the remaining 97 percent combined.

As mentioned at the beginning of the book, setting goals is the same as laying out a good road map for your life. The first phase is to find exactly where you are now, the second is to determine where you want to go, and the third is to pick the easiest route that will take you there.

The next exercise deals with the first phase: "You are here."

You Are Here

The Law of Talents states that *you contain within yourself a unique combination of talents and abilities, which, properly identified and applied, will enable you to achieve virtually any goal you can set for yourself.*

What parts of your work do you enjoy the most and are you the best at? This is your best indicator of your true talents.

The secret to powerful and effective goals is some form of visualization. Visualize the answer to each of the questions that follow, making the answers as specific as possible.

This exercise will establish the starting point: this is the point separating those who truly want to make a change from those who are still afraid. Those who do will fill the following pages and more. Those who are still afraid to will find a dozen good reasons for not doing so. Are you still afraid that if you write these things down, someone will find them and judge you? Are you afraid you may have to become accountable? Are you afraid you might fail?

You are not alone. This is the big step. This is the leap that will take you from where you are now to accomplishing your wildest dreams. What is the price of that fear if you hold back now? My first employer was extremely successful at an early age, so much so that *Reader's Digest* ran a story on him. Then, in the early 1980s, our city's economy collapsed, and many of the local businesses failed, including his. I remember some jealous people saying nasty things, making fun of his fall and the new dreams he was not afraid to share, and the positive attitude he wore as he began again.

He was not afraid to help others, including myself, with moral support, encouraging us to get back on our feet, but he did take flak from some for having the courage to move forward in a time of fear. He recently sold out his businesses and retired a very wealthy man. Now we work on projects together just for fun and extra profit. I asked him how he got through those rough days when a lot of people seemed to be taking potshots at him, and he said, "Dogs only bark at moving cars." If no one is barking at you, you may feel safe, but it is a sure sign you are not moving. Thanks, Fred, for thirty-five years of encouragement. I look forward to moving right on alongside you for at least thirty-five more.

There are people out there willing to help *you* achieve your goals and dreams as well. Ignore the barking dogs and find the leaders to run with. They are the only ones who will end up somewhere, and most are more than happy to have you run alongside.

Real leaders don't care what you think about them or their dreams. Leaders focus only on what they wish to accomplish. They welcome those who wish to join them on their journey and realize that, out of ignorance and fear, there will be those who oppose them, make fun of them, or just don't understand what is going to be achieved. But that is those other people's problem.

It is time to risk the challenges of leadership. Complete the following: List ten of your natural talents and abilities. We are taught not to brag about our talents or abilities, but even the Bible tells us not to hide our light under a bushel. We are all unique, and you have some talents and abilities that give you a distinct advantage. What are they?

1. _____

2. _____

3. _____

4. _____

5. _____

6. _____

7. _____

8. _____

9. _____

10. _____

What five things have been responsible for your success in life so far? No matter where in the life cycle you are, you have already experienced some successes. What allowed you to achieve those successes?

1. _____

2. _____

3. _____

4. _____

5. _____

What five things hold your attention and interest? Don't evaluate whether they are of any economic value or whether you can use them to make a living; just list them. What is it you really like?

1. _____

2. _____

3. _____

4. _____

5. _____

List your five basic, most important values and virtues. Some people have an insatiable appetite for knowledge, others for social causes. Some are driven by beauty and harmony while still others want a good return on their time and resources. Some people value their spirituality or religion while others just want to be independent, and the list goes on. What is driving you?

1. _____

2. _____

3. _____

4. _____

5. _____

List the ten activities that give you the greatest feeling of importance. Many of us try to hide our ego, as if it is something to be ashamed
of, yet deep inside most of us crave some attention or the feeling some
power gives us. We all want to feel like we are making a difference. What
gives you a feeling of importance?

1. _____

2. _____

3. _____

4. _____

5. _____

6. _____

7. _____

8. _____

9. _____

10. _____

List the ten things you most liked to do between the ages of ten
and fifteen. (Ask your parents if you need to.) Some people turn their
childhood dreams into successful life pursuits while others are discouraged, much like my older football-playing friend, and build their lives
on someone else's idea of what they should do. I know many grown-up
people who still play kids' games for a living. I loved to write as a child
but became convinced that I could not make a living at it, so I hid that
dream away for over thirty years before I discovered I could do what
I like and make money too. What are the things you used to love doing?

1. _____

2. _____

3. _____

4. _____

5. _____

6. _____

7. _____

8. _____

9. _____

10. _____

List ten things you always wanted to do in life but have been afraid to attempt. Again, this is a difficult thing to do the first time. I was fortunate in that I made a list a long time ago and have since crossed off many items, including flying my own plane across the U.S., traveling to remote parts of the world, and speaking widely in public, but let me share with you some of the things still on my list: I would like to act in a play or movie, and I would like to take singing lessons. There it is. I told the world. Now you can risk writing your ideas here in the privacy of this book.

1. _____

2. _____

3. _____

4. _____

5. _____

6. _____

7. _____

8. _____

9. _____

10. _____

Keeping in mind the SMART formula for goal setting (that is, make them Specific, Measurable, Attainable, Realistic, and Timely), list the three most important goals you have in life right now.

1. _____

_____

2. _____

_____

3. _____

_____

What four things would you do today if you knew you only had six months to live? When death looks us in the eye, as it will all of us eventually, we suddenly realize where our priorities should have been. If you had it to live over, would you have put in the extra time to make a few more dollars, or would you have taken the time to see your son or daughter play their favorite game or participated in some other event that made you happy? What new priorities would you suddenly have if you realized your time were limited? It's time to quit fooling yourself . . . your time *is* limited. You may only have six hours, six days, six months, six years, or six decades left. Who knows? Why risk losing another day? What are the four most important things you want to do?

1. _____

_____

2. _____

_____

3. _____

_____

4. _____

_____

How would your life change if you won a million dollars tax-free? What three things would you do right away?

1. _____

_____

2. _____

_____

3. _____

_____

(Now, do you really need the money, or is not having it just an excuse not to risk going for what you really want?)

What is your major purpose in life? Don't be discouraged. This will take some time and introspection. Don't rush it. Myrna knew immediately what her purpose was, as it came to her in a flash. I, on the other hand, am still wrestling with this question.

_____

_____

_____

_____

_____

Congratulations! You have just completed a session on mind mapping, a voyage of discovery in identifying who you really are and what you really want. This is not an easy task, so don't be surprised if you have to do it a few times before it feels right.

The purpose of these exercises is to help you gain a clearer picture of what your talents and desires really are. Your answers also give you some insights into areas where you may need some additional instruction or practice. When analyzing where you are, do not forget that you don't have to stay there. Don't listen to your inner voice or anyone else when deciding what you are capable of. There are great examples in life of supposed experts and their predictions:

"We don't like their sound, and guitar music is on the way out." This memo was sent by a senior vice president from Decca Recording Company, rejecting the Beatles in 1962. How much do you think that limiting belief cost Decca? If an expert can be that far off, so can anyone else. Be like the Beatles and stay focused.

"I have traveled the length and breadth of this country and talked with the best people, and I can assure you that data processing is a fad that won't last out the year." This statement came from the editor in charge of business books for Prentice Hall in 1957.

"There is no reason anyone would want a computer in their home." Ken Olson, president, chairman, and founder of Digital Equipment Corporation, said this in 1977. Fewer than thirty years later, I am trying to decide which of the four computers we have in our home I should use.

"640K ought to be enough for anybody." Bill Gates, 1981, apocryphal, speaking of the amount of memory for a personal computer. Bill, what were you thinking?

"This 'telephone' has too many shortcomings to be seriously considered as a means of communication. The device is inherently of no value to us." This Western Union internal memo of 1876 shows how when we focus only on our own interests, we are sometimes blinded to other possibilities. Western Union had telegraph posts and employees strung across the nation, and with very little effort could have been the first major telephone company.

"The wireless music box has no imaginable commercial value. Who would pay for a message sent to nobody in particular?" This is how David Sarnoff's associates responded to his urgings for investment in the radio in the 1920s.

"Heavier-than-air flying machines are impossible." Lord Kelvin, president of the Royal Society, made this prediction in 1895, fewer than ten years before the Wright brothers' first flight.

"So we went to Atari and said, 'Hey, we've got this amazing thing, even built with some of your parts, and what do you think about funding us? Or we'll give it to you. We just want to do it. Pay our salary, we'll come work for you.'

And they said, 'No.' So then we went to Hewlett-Packard, and they said, 'Hey, we don't need you. You haven't got through college yet.'" Apple Computer founder Steve Jobs said this about the attempts to get Atari and HP interested in his and Steve Wozniak's personal computer. Fortunately, they did not buy into the comment that they did not have the education required. In fact, had they a formal education in the subject, they probably would have learned that they were going in the wrong direction. Often, great things are accomplished by people who didn't learn it can't be done.

"If I had thought about it, I wouldn't have done the experiment. The literature was full of examples that said you can't do this." Spencer Silver on the work that led to the unique adhesives for 3M's Post-It sticky notes.

Search out biographies or stories about similar people with similar circumstances to yours and use them as inspiration to keep you moving in the direction you want to go.

As a writer, my editors, readers, and friends often critique what I write, and sometimes critics or reviewers are harsh, making my inner voice ask the question, "Layton, what are you doing? Who do you think you are, anyway? What makes you think you have something important to say?" To remind myself how much value I should put on their opinions, I keep the following quotes nearby:

"I am sorry, Mr. Kipling, but you just do not know how to use the English language." This statement was made to Rudyard Kipling by the *San Francisco Examiner* in a rejection letter in 1889.

"Shakespeare's name, you may depend on it, will go down. He has no invention as to stories, none whatever." Lord Byron said this about the Bard in 1814.

"We fancy that any child might be more puzzled than enchanted by this stiff, silly, overwrought story." The quote comes from a *Children's Books* review from 1865. The story was *Alice in Wonderland*, by Lewis Carroll.

twenty-three

Your Future Looks Great!

The Law of Indirect Effort states that *you will be more successful indirectly in relationships than directly. To have a friend, be a friend. To impress others, be impressed by them. To develop and maintain loving relationships, become a loving person yourself.*

Project yourself into the future and describe your perfect world. This description should include personal items, people, shapes, sounds, smells, colors, and textures. Stretch your mind! The more clearly you visualize your goals, the quicker they will appear. Describe everything in your perfect environment. You may want to begin a separate notebook in order to have lots of room for this exercise.

Just let the words flow. Don't evaluate or use your rational conscious mind to analyze each item. Just write them as they come to you.

My new home is approximately _____ square feet and is located in

the city of _____, where I now live. The home is

best described as _____

_____

_____

_____

The car I drive is a (color, make, and model) _____

_____

_____

When I drive it I feel _____

_____

_____

The things I now do for recreation and enjoyment include:

1. _____

2. _____

3. _____

4. _____

5. _____

6. _____

7. _____

8. _____

I have now visited all the places I've dreamed of, including the top twenty-five listed here:

(*Example—I ran through Stanley Park in Vancouver, British Columbia.*)

1. _____

2. _____

3. _____

4. _____

5. _____

6. _____

7. _____

8. _____

9. _____

10. _____

11. _____

12. _____

13. _____

14. _____

15. _____

16. _____

17. _____

18. _____

19. _____

20. _____

21. _____

22. _____

23. _____

24. _____

25. _____

Career and Professional Development

The Law of Maximization states that *you always try to get the very most in exchange for your time, money, effort, or emotions. When given a choice between more or less for the same contribution, you will always choose more. People are greedy in everything they do. This is neither good nor bad in itself. It just is.*

There is a story about the old trapper who froze to death because he kept saying to his stove, "If you give me more heat, I will give you more wood." We all recognize this as a silly story, yet there are two schools of thought that people bring to the workplace. In one, people heap on the wood by giving whatever task they are assigned their full and best effort in the expectation that they will be rewarded with more heat (money or promotions).

The workers who belong to the second school often ridicule those of the first school and, like the foolish old trapper, say, "Give me more heat (money or promotions) and I will give you more wood (produce more)." These people are often upset at business owners because they seem to favor those other guys, but why should they put out a ten-dollar effort if they are only getting a five-dollar salary?

I recently ran into another hockey dad I know from the rink and asked him how things were going. He replied that they were not good, as he had just been laid off.

"Downsizing?" I asked.

"That's what they called it," he said. "But the boss arranged it so he could keep the company sucks working and laid off a few of us who were telling him if he paid us more, we would we would work a lot more effective. We also told him lots of other ways he could run his company better." The boss may not have been the best businessperson in the city, who knows, but this fellow didn't seem to understand that there is a reason why he was just a worker and the boss ran the place.

Some people think that all employers only take advantage of people and will not automatically reward them for their efforts. In the short term, they may be right. But of course, business owners and managers are always looking to improve their businesses, and they know that if they don't promote or give raises to the best workers, they will lose them to a competitor. When times get tough, it is the best they keep. This is a basic flaw in union agreements: they treat all workers the same, so all workers slowly become the same, and the trend is to become like the lowest common denominator, meeting only the minimum expectations. Those who follow this trend become the workers who remain behind, while those who work hard end up being promoted out of the union and into management.

Don't be afraid to break away from the pack mentality and set your own pace. To do that effectively, project yourself into the future and list the desirable aspects of your now-perfect professional life. Describe the type of work you do, the level of prestige you reach, the level of stress you have, and the challenges and recognition you achieve. Think about income levels, personal satisfaction, and other rewards. In your wildest dreams, you would never have dared to think this big, but now it is all yours!

Complete the following sentences for five and ten years out. Revisit and rewrite your answers every three months.

My career now consists of _____

_____

_____

_____

_____

_____

_____

The salary and benefits I get include _____

_____

_____

_____

_____

People whom I have had the pleasure to meet and who have influenced my career include _____

_____

_____

_____

_____

_____

_____

"You can't steal second base and keep your foot on first."

—Frederick Wilcox

The Law of Attraction states that *you attract into your life the people, ideas, and opportunities that harmonize with your dominant thoughts. When your goals are magnetized with the emotion of desire, you will experience what others call "luck."*

Get around the right people. We take on the behavior of those around us. Associate with winners and eagles.

List both those special people you want to have close relationships with as well as those you would like to get to know. Also, give a timeline for meeting them. We should all be in constant search of new friends and relationships. It is just as difficult or takes just as much work to meet and become friends with people who can influence your personal and business life as it does to make friends with those who can't. I am not suggesting that you become a social climber or only welcome important or influential people into your life, however. Welcome all who will come, as everyone has value as long as they bring with them a positive and healthy mental attitude. There is an old saying that if you look at who your friends are, you will see who you are going to be in the near future. Negativity breeds negativity and brings destruction into your mental thinking. As much as you may wish to rescue some good folks from their state of negativity, you cannot help them until they are ready. In the meantime, avoid them, as they will bring you down. If you are going to target folks to be friends with, why not be friends with positive, like-minded people who can truly help you reach your goals?

You will also find you can establish closer, deeper relationships with these like-minded people. If you cannot name them specifically, then describe who they are, what values they will have, what income brackets they will be in, what types of positions they will hold, and so on.

Example—Build a closer relationship with my children over the next year.

Example—Meet Bill Gates, Seattle, 2008.

_____

_____

_____

_____

_____

_____

_____

_____

_____

_____

_____

_____

_____

_____

_____

_____

_____

"Chance favors the prepared mind."

—Louis Pasteur

Relationships

The Law of Relationships states that *the more people you know and who know you in a positive way, the luckier you will be. People will give you ideas and open doors for you if they like you.*

I have included a few exercises here around friends and relationships, because that is really the measure of true wealth and happiness. Bear with me, remembering that repetition is a key ingredient to reprogramming the subconscious mind. How many friends and acquaintances do you want? What qualities or values do you want them to have? Who are these people? What do you want in your family or intimate relationships? Be clear, be specific, and ask for what you really want.

In 1908, Napoleon Hill was commissioned by Andrew Carnegie, then the richest man in the world, to interview the 504 most successful people of the time and find what they had in common.

His findings resulted in the book *Think and Grow Rich*, published in 1937, which outlined the "13 Principles" identified as being common to every successful person.

One of the keys was that they all belonged to "Master Mind" groups, which Hill interpreted as meaning that no successful person does it alone. These successful people all surrounded themselves with people who could help them, inspire them, advise them, criticize them, encourage them, and motivate them to be better than they could be on their own.

Hill also suggested that people working in a Master Mind group could tap into the universal intelligence. He said that two or more minds coming together to focus on a single purpose causes an infusion of intellect that is not achieved by the individuals alone.

Complete the following sentence: The six close business friends who are all a part of my Master Mind group are . . .

Five years from today: _____

_____

_____

_____

_____

_____

Ten years from today: _____

_____

_____

_____

_____

_____

_____

A good friend of mine, who is still an active and very successful businessman despite being well into his eighties, had this bit of advice: "At the end of your days, if you can count five or six really close friends, you are indeed well off." I know of hundreds of people who also consider him a good friend and like and respect him, but he knows the difference between a good friend and a very close friend, and he values the latter above all else.

When I think about the dozens of people I consider my good friends, there are four who stand out above all the rest. These people would rally to my aid without question. I am still always looking for similar people to make new friends with, because I know as we travel through life that circumstances and good friends sometimes change. In fact, in addition to these four people, four more have been great close friends of mine in the past, but for one reason or another, we have not been in touch much lately. It is interesting how we never lose these people, and often they cycle back into our lives several times, becoming close, then drifting away for a while, and then returning. It is almost as though we are all separate planets in our own orbits: sometimes we travel close to one another, and sometimes we don't but know that we will again. I feel very rich for having these people in my life. I encourage you to spend some time considering this exercise very seriously, because, as my senior friend says, "In the end, it is your friends that really count."

I can count on these people to come to my assistance without question. If you don't have these people now, who would you like them to be? If not specific names or relationships, what characteristics would they have?

_____

_____

_____

The organizations you belong to also determine your relationships. What organizations you would like to be involved with? List at least three, along with your reasons for wanting to be involved.

Example—Rotary: to give back to the community in a meaningful way, make friends in the business community, and have more social opportunities for my family to participate in.

_____

_____

_____

_____

_____

_____

"The difference between success and failure is not a lack of strength, knowledge, or skill, but a lack of will."

—Unknown

Spirituality, Wellness, and Self-Expression

The Law of Integrity states that *happiness and high performance come to you when you choose to live your life consistently with your highest values and your deepest convictions.*

Always be true to the very best that is within you.

Describe or express your innermost values. What do you want more of in your life? What will have to change for you to take perfect care of your mental, emotional, physical, and spiritual well-being? What will assist you in being (or becoming) completely and fully alive as a person?

I was sent to Sunday school at a Presbyterian Church but quit attending when I left school. For years, if I was asked what religion I was, I would respond, "Presbyterian." Then I met and fell in love with Myrna, a practicing Catholic, so when we decided to be married, I converted. After we left our old community, we had trouble feeling welcome in the new church and were disturbed by much of what was going on within it, so we drifted away.

Over the years that followed, I began to think about the Creator, spirituality, and how we are all connected. One day, after a limited first version of this book was released, I got a call from a man who said he had read the book and really wanted to talk to me about it. When he arrived at my office, his first question was, "Are you a student of Phineas Parkhurst Quimby?"

"A student? I never heard of the guy," I replied. "Who is he?"

"He was a hypnotist who lived in the 1800s and traveled the West. His writings have resulted in him being called 'the Father of New Thought.'" He went on to say that much of what I have written here appears to have been quoted from Quimby's writings. I assured him that I had never heard of him before, so he told me how several churches based on his work had been established. The churches he belonged to, the Center for Positive Living and the Science of the Mind Church, were basically Christian churches but believed that Christ was here to teach us how to access the universal intelligence, the Ultimate All-Knowing, or God, through the thoughts in our subconscious mind. "Interesting," I thought, "a religious movement based on the same theories of the mind that I find so powerful." We finished our stimulating conversation, and after he left, I checked the Internet to see what else good old Phineas may have had to say on the subject. What I found was very interesting, as the opening line read, "Phineas Parkhurst Quimby, who was known as 'Park,' was born on February 16, 1802, in Lebanon, New Hampshire, and died on January 16, 1866, in Belfast, Maine, where he lived most of his life."

"Park," I thought. "He not only was writing the same thoughts but he was doing so under the same name." I felt as though the music from *The Twilight Zone* should begin.

That exchange has caused me to re-examine my spiritual beliefs, which by my definition do not necessarily mean my religious affiliations. In my case, I believe that the key to life is in living the golden rule, and everything else is just commentary.

Complete the following sentence: Five new beliefs or practices that I now have in my life include . . .

1. _____

2. _____

3. _____

4. _____

5. _____

"Health is the first wealth."

—Ralph Waldo Emerson

What do you really want for your life? You've thought about and described your home and personal environment. You've defined your ideal work and career and reviewed the relationships you want in your life. You've taken time to think about your values, spirituality, health, and well-being. What does it all add up to?

_____

_____

_____

_____

_____

In the space on the next page, review the things you've written on the preceding pages and think about how you would like to summarize your biggest dreams and your most important desires. Describe your perfect life. Remember, do not let self-doubt enter into this exercise, and do not beat yourself up for past experiences that did not turn out the way you would have liked them to. Use positive affirmations to remove all negative thoughts from your mind.

As Vince Lombardi once said, "I have never lost a game, but sometimes I may have run out of time." The past does not equal the future, so let your imagination run wild. Anything you can conceive and believe, you can achieve. In this step, you are only conceiving the future you truly desire.

_____

_____

_____

_____

_____

_____

_____

_____

_____

_____

_____

_____

_____

_____

_____

_____

_____

_____

_____

"To think is to practice brain chemistry."

—Deepak Chopra

What to Do Now

The Law of Reality states that *people don't change. Deal with them as they are. Don't try to change others or expect them to change. "What you see is what you get."*

Unconditional acceptance of others is the key to happy relationships.

Your goals are a directive to your subconscious mind, and it is a genius at getting them for you! Begin now by reviewing these pages often, and do not become discouraged if at first you do not appear to be heading in the right direction. Keep the vision, keep the faith, and all will unfold the way you have planned.

The most effective way to truly change your thinking and open up your reticular activating system is to take one or two pages, go to a quiet room, and put yourself into a light hypnotic state. The enclosed CD will teach you how to do this quickly and effectively. Once in this state, play a movie in your mind in which you see, hear, smell, and feel yourself having already achieved these goals. This is very similar to a daydream in which you suspend your critical thinking and allow yourself just to see your life unfold perfectly. The more you witness this, the more your subconscious mind will begin to accept it as the truth.

For example, think of five things you will do today to begin moving in the direction of your future. They may be very small things (like cleaning the garage or balancing the checkbook), but they tell your mind you are serious about heading down this new path.

After setting my goals, in the first twenty-four hours I accomplished:

1. _____

2. _____

3. _____

4. _____

5. _____

"All things are difficult before they are easy."

—John Norley

During the next thirty days, I completed the following:

1. _____

2. _____

3. _____

4. _____

5. _____

6. _____

7. _____

8. _____

9. _____

10. _____

"To stay the course, sometimes you have to make waves."

—Unknown

First-Year Report

Continue following the basic actions laid out in your plans to move forward every day. They do not have to be dramatic, difficult, or dangerous. Make the bed, lose a pound a week, save a hundred dollars per month, or read one hour a day. Commit to taking the small steps that over time will complete the journey of a thousand miles. Follow the path that will create the future you want.

List the specific, measurable commitments for the first year of the program. What things need to be learned, changed, or implemented in order to move your life from where it was to where you planned for it to be at the end of year one? Be honest. Be specific. Be clear.

Example—I cleaned and organized the garage and basement so I can find things, and it no longer frustrates me to go in there.

Example—I finished taking extra evening courses so I could apply for a higher position in the company.

By the end of the first year, I completed or achieved:

_____

_____

_____

_____

_____

_____

_____

_____

_____

_____

_____

"True success is overcoming the fear of being unsuccessful."

—Paul Sweeney

Fifty Things to Do Before I Die

Every year, Myrna and I review our year and lay out new goals. Often, we bring new tools or ideas that may assist us in making our plans clearer. One fun exercise we have done for a number of years with some good friends is to create a list of fifty things to do before we die. It is a lot of fun to sit down each year, cross off the things we accomplished since we last met, and replace them with new things. Make your own list. Be bold! Itemize some of the craziest things that you want to do. Let your imagination run wild.

It was while doing this exercise that I listed traveling to a former Soviet country for free. A short time later, I was introduced to CESO (Canadian Executive Service Organization). I joined, and the first place I was sent as a volunteer, to consult to an architectural and engineering company, was Almaty, Kazakhstan. That trip made me some good friends who I still keep in touch with, and it also resulted in a very well-paid contract that returned me to Kazakhstan two years later.

Each year I am surprised at how many things can be crossed off the list, especially when I never consciously thought about them. I was just ready to take advantage of the opportunities as they appeared.

Some of the other examples from my list include:

Ski fifty different mountains

Cruise the Nile with four friends

Give my favorite charity $100,000

Go ahead, get a couple of friends together and make your own list. You will find the first dozen or so easy, and then eventually you will be forced to really think, "What would I really like to do?"

1. _____

2. _____

3. _____

4. _____

5. _____

6. _____

7. _____

8. _____

9. _____

10. _____

11. _____

12. _____

13. _____

14. _____

15. _____

16. _____

17. _____

18. _____

19. _____

20. _____

21. _____

22. _____

23. _____

24. _____

25. _____

26. _____

27. _____

28. _____

29. _____

30. _____

31. _____

32. _____

33. _____

34. _____

35. _____

36. _____

37. _____

38. _____

39. _____

40. _____

41. _____

42. _____

43. _____

44. _____

45. _____

46. _____

47. _____

48. _____

49. _____

50. _____

"Gold is where you find it!"

—Midge Westermark

twenty-four

Gaining Clarity

Most successful people will agree that they owe their success to their ability to set and achieve goals.

The key to success is in setting goals. We are encouraged to set goals personally, as family members, as community members, as team members, and as company employees. We are encouraged to set financial goals, sales goals, and physical-conditioning goals. Some goal-setting experts claim you should have a limited number of focused goals, while other speakers suggest that the more goals the better, so long as they are not in conflict with each other.

Regardless of which school of thought you follow, it is important to remember that if your goals are registered or imprinted on the brain, they become important and the opportunities that will lead to their accomplishment will suddenly materialize. Opportunities will seem to appear everywhere, and obtaining the goals will become easier for you.

Another technique used for setting goals, which may assist you, is the collage or storyboard. This is done by cutting out pictures or graphics of various goals and pasting them together. I never understood the importance of this exercise until I studied how the brain works. If you recall, the left side of the brain is our logical side. When we traditionally set goals, we write them in a logical or left-brain order. If we wish to make the process more powerful, then we need to engage both sides of the brain. The right side of the brain deals primarily in images and pictures, thus the reason for viewing the goals in a graphic or picture format. The problem is that most of the boards tend to look as though they were put together by a left-brain artist, if there is such a thing. As most people are predominately left-brained, they use a graphic format but lay out the collage in a nice, neat, logical manner. The suggestion has been made that to really get the right brain involved, large pieces of paper should be used and the goals should be creatively drawn. Regardless of artistic ability, or lack thereof, it is more powerful to have a self-produced drawing of the new Mercedes looking like a pumpkin on wheels than it is to have a full-color glossy photo. In fact, the more you have to engage your imagination to see the object, the better it registers in your subconscious mind.

Draw the most important goals the largest and the least important the smallest. Remember, less is more, so these don't have to be well-detailed renderings. Simple line drawings that the imagination can use to identify the object are more than adequate. This exercise will get the right side of the brain building the same goals as the left side of the brain, and the results will be more powerful.

In the early 1960s, the United States had just put its first man into space but was losing the space race overall. The young new president, John F. Kennedy, promised the American people that they would put a man on the moon before the end of the decade. He didn't lay out a program saying that by next year they had to circle the globe and the year after they would have to develop this or that; he just set the vision and then got out of the way. The vision outlived the visionary. Very little of the technology required to send a man to the moon and bring him back safely existed when President Kennedy made the commitment. In fact, American experts weren't sure what all would be needed or how they would go about doing it. The vision was clear, however, and was sent out to the people who in eight short years accomplished the feat.

If the vision is clear, the mind will begin the process of moving toward the goal. Let the subconscious mind lead, follow intuition or the gut feeling, and don't let the ever-analyzing conscious mind develop reasons why it can't be done. That is not to say we set a goal and then sit back and wait. Once the vision has been set, we have to take actions to ensure that we continue moving toward that goal.

It's time to begin.

When Myrna managed the real-estate company, she would not hire anyone who said they wanted to "try selling real estate." She would say to them, "Either you are going to sell real estate or you are not. If you are willing to work at becoming a Realtor, then welcome aboard. If you are only going to 'try,' then we just don't have room for you on our team right now." It is a Realtor's job to *sell* homes, not *show* them.

The language we use is as important as the message it conveys to the subconscious. Remember, to use the word "try" is to ask in advance for forgiveness for failing. For example, if I say I will "try" to meet you for lunch tomorrow and then I don't show up, I already have my excuse ready. I don't have to feel guilty, because I did say I would try. I tried, but somehow I didn't make it—sorry.

We are not planning to set goals that we may or may not achieve; we are here to set a course for where we plan to go. To use "try" is to set ourselves up for failure, and it is a first cousin to "setting" goals. To only "set" goals is not making enough of a commitment to obtaining them.

From now on, let's not *set* goals. Let's go *get* goals, keeping in mind that "persistence is self-discipline in motion." Just as inertia applies to Newton's first law of motion in the physical world, it also applies to the mental world. This law states: "An object at rest tends to stay at rest, and an object in motion tends to stay in motion with the same speed and in the same direction unless acted upon by an unbalanced force." Once you begin moving toward your goal, you will find it is easy to stay in motion.

Attitude Is a Reflection of Leadership

Business surveys rate attitude as the number one trait for success among leaders. Attitude controls our actions, and our actions determine the results. Do you have a good attitude about what you can expect from these exercises? Remember the Law of Expectations, which says you will receive from this book exactly what you expect to receive. I have had dozens of letters and e-mails in support of this material and telling of the results others have had with its use. I know some will approach it with a negative attitude and find they only get negative results. Make sure you approach this book with the attitude of a leader. Use it yourself, and when you see the results, encourage your subordinates to get their own copies or send in for a bulk order and give a copy to everyone on your team. You will find it does not cost your company money, because if only one employee embraces it and improves his or her performance, it will yield larger results than the few dollars the book and CD costs.

It seems reasonable to think that leaders would strive to instill good attitudes in their people, but when that does not happen, who is responsible? Attitude is a reflection of leadership. Or, as Myrna says, "A fish stinks from the head."

As a leader, this can be a bitter pill to swallow. Most of us are eager to accept credit for the great attitude that surrounds our people when things are going well. However, when they aren't, it irritates us to have someone dare suggest that the attitude of those we lead is somehow a refection on our own abilities. After all, isn't everyone responsible for choosing their own attitude?

The truth is, they are, but a leader motivates them to make the right choice. If others in the organization are causing attitude problems, then it becomes a failure of the leader if he or she does not deal with them. The leader must take responsibility for the general attitude of the organization he or she leads, or, as President John F. Kennedy once said, "If not us, who?"

The good news is that once leaders understand this to be true, they can make the choices and changes necessary to create their vision of the future.

Most people become leaders because they have a vision and possess a great deal of knowledge and skill to make that vision real. The largest challenge they report is to achieve and maintain the right attitude in their followers in order to produce results they desire. While some leaders seem to have a natural charisma that allows them to lead in a seemingly effortless manner while people follow along behind, others feel as though they are herding chickens. Studies show that the difference between good leaders and great leaders is insignificant and that most leadership skills can be learned, so why are there not more great leaders?

The key is in learning to think differently about our talents and abilities, developing winning edges, and mastering the skills of other high achievers in clearly visualizing the future with the results we desire.

This book can help you a great deal in moving in that same direction, but you did not learn the habits you have now overnight and it will take more than a quick reading of this book to change them.

I encourage you to really give this an honest effort and then send me notes outlining the exciting results you've discovered.

Congratulations

You have designed the beginning of a plan that, once fully developed, will bring immense joy to your life.

Repeat this program often. Every navigator knows that there have to be occasional course corrections. Look at any changes, retrim the sails, make the adjustments, and continue sailing toward the life you really want.

You can adjust or change your answers as often as appropriate. You know what you want, and you are in control!

The saddest words in the English language are "If I had only . . ."

You can accomplish anything you put your mind to.

Everyone has a seed of greatness in them, and it will take sprout and grow with just a little nourishment and encouragement. All you have to do is truly decide what you want . . . then get out of your way.

appendix

Self-Hypnosis CD
with Layton Park

Introduction

Psychologists generally agree that we each hold core beliefs about our abilities and ourselves. We then tend to act in accordance with our beliefs, and the results we obtain in life are a direct result of our actions.

The way to change yourself and your actions is to change your core beliefs. Use the audio CD accompanying this book, featuring the following personal guided hypnosis by hypnotherapist Layton Park, at least once per day, and you will see the changes you desire.

Self-Hypnosis for Achieving Your Goals

I want you to begin by looking up at the ceiling, picking a spot on the ceiling, and focusing on it for the next few minutes.

As you focus on that spot, I want you to take nice, deep breaths all the way in and all the way out, and with every breath I want you to allow your body to relax more and more. With every breath in and every breath out, allow yourself to go deeper and deeper into relaxation. Continue to focus on the spot. As you focus on the spot, you will notice in a moment that your eyes will begin to feel strained. They may begin to feel heavy. They may feel so tired that you want to close them, and if they do, that's all right.

You may close them, and continue to breathe all the way in, all the way out. You may also notice that the spot begins to go out of focus or your eyes begin to water. That's perfectly natural; don't strain them. Whenever any of these things happen or whenever you feel as though you would be more comfortable with your eyes closed, please close your eyes and continue to breathe all the way in, all the way out.

Allow yourself to go deeper and deeper into relaxation. Allow yourself to go deeper and deeper, relaxing more and more with every breath, all the way in, all the way out. Allow yourself to go deeper and deeper and deeper.

That's right: just keep breathing nice and deep, all the way in, all the way out. And what we are going to do to begin with is called the Progressive Body of Relaxation, in which I am going to describe different muscle groups in your body. And as you breathe in and out, I want you to visualize in your mind these muscle groups. I want you to see them as clearly as you can, and as you breathe in, I want you to tighten every muscle in that muscle group up as tight as you can and hold it as you hold your breath. Then, as you release your breath, release the muscles and feel them become more and more relaxed. We are going to move through your entire body, relaxing each and every muscle group in your body until you feel totally relaxed.

I want you to begin with your toes. In your mind, I want you to see your toes. See each and every little toe, each and every muscle in every toe. Now, as you see them clearly in your mind, take a nice, deep breath in, and as you do, tighten those muscles up and hold them, and as you release your breath all the way out, relax your toes. Feel how relaxed your toes become. Allow all stress, worry, and tension to drain from your toes right out the tips of your toes and away. Just allow all tension, stress, and worry to drain away . . . drain away . . . drain away.

Now I want you to see each and every muscle in the tops of your feet, the bottoms of your feet, your arches, your heels, all the muscles in your feet, all the muscles in your ankles, and as you breathe in a nice, deep breath all the way in, tighten each and every muscle up as tight as you can, and hold it, hold it, hold it, and release it, let them go.

See all those muscles become loose, limp, and relaxed. See all that tension, stress, and worry draining from your feet, down through your toes, out the tips, and away, and you feel yourself becoming more and more relaxed. You feel yourself going deeper and deeper into relaxation.

Now, all the muscles in your legs, starting in your ankles, all the muscles in your calves and your shins and your knees. All the muscles in your thighs, right up to your hips, see each and every muscle, see them clearly in your mind, and as you breathe in, breathe in all the way, tightening each and every muscle. Hold it and release them, release your breath, release the muscles, and feel all that stress, worry, and tension draining from your legs, down through your feet, out your toes, and away. You feel your whole lower body becoming more and more relaxed. You feel your legs becoming heavier and heavier and heavier as you slip into a deeper and deeper state of relaxation, going deeper and deeper. Now all the muscles in your upper body, starting with the muscles in the pit of your stomach, right through to the small of your back, all the muscles up your backbone, over your shoulders and into your chest. See each and every muscle clearly in your mind. As you breathe in, breathe all the way in, hold it, tighten them, hold it, release them, let them go. Let your breath go all the way out. Feel all that tension, stress, and worry draining from your upper body, down through your lower body, through your feet, out your toes, and away. And you go deeper and deeper, deeper and deeper.

Now all the muscles in your fingers and your thumbs, all the muscles in the palms of your hands and the back of your hands, all the muscles in your wrists. See each and every little muscle in your mind as you breathe in. Tighten each and every muscle up and hold it, and as you breathe out, release them, let them go. Feel all the tension, stress, and worry draining from your hands right down through your fingers and out your fingertips and away, and you feel yourself going deeper and deeper and becoming more and more relaxed.

Now all the muscles in your arms, from your wrist to your shoulders, all the muscles in your forearms and your upper arms. As you breathe in, see each and every muscle tighten up. Tighten them as tight as you can, hold them for a second, then release them, relax them, let them go.

Let all that tension, stress, and worry drain from your arms down through your hands, out your fingertips and away, and you feel your entire body relaxing more and more. With every breath out, you feel more and more relaxed, more relaxed than before, your arms beginning to feel so heavy, so very, very heavy. Your entire body sinking deeper and deeper into the chair, your entire body relaxing more and more. That's right: just allow yourself, allow yourself to drift deeper and deeper, just let go and allow yourself to go deeper and deeper.

Now all the muscles in your throat, all the muscles along your jaw line, where your jaw connects to your skull, at the base of your ear. See those muscles in your mind, all the muscles at the base of your skull, all the little muscles around your mouth, all the muscles in the lower part of your face and neck. See each and every muscle clearly in your mind. Then, as you breathe in, tighten them and hold them, and then as you breathe out, release them and let them go. Let them go completely. See yourself relaxing more and more.

Now, finally, all the muscles in your upper face and head, starting with the muscles deep in your eyes. Feel all the muscles in your eyes, in your eyelids, your eyebrows, your eyelashes, all the muscles in the bridge of your nose, each and every little muscle in your forehead, all the muscles in the upper part of your cheeks and your ears, every little muscle in your scalp. See all these muscles clearly in your mind. See them clearly as you breathe in, and tighten them, and then, as you breathe out, release them and let them go, and feel the stress, tension, and worry draining from your upper head, down through your lower head and jaw, through your upper body, your lower body, your legs, your feet, your toes, and away.

See it just draining away, draining away, your entire body going deeper and deeper, feeling more and more relaxed. That's right, just continue to drift downward, going deeper and deeper, becoming more and more relaxed, sinking further and further into the chair. It's as though your body is getting heavier and heavier. With every breath, your body becomes heavier and heavier, but your mind is beginning to float. Your mind is beginning to break free and float. It's as though your mind is like a leaf, a leaf on a stream just floating along on the surface, just drifting along so light as your body sinks deeper and deeper. It's as though your mind is breaking free and floating while your body sinks deeper into the chair, becoming more and more relaxed . . . more and more relaxed.

Now, in your mind, I want you to picture a clock. This clock is a huge clock, two or three times larger than you are, and as you stare at it, you notice that it has a white face and big black numbers. And as you stare at it, you are going to notice as I call out each number that it falls off the face of the clock and then just disappears, just fades away, leaving behind a white spot where the number once was. And as I count down all the numbers and they continue to fall off the face and fade away, you will finally be left with just the white face, a white face that you will continue to stare at. And as I count down each number, I am going to tell you to go to sleep, deep, deep asleep . . . but we know it's not sleep like you experience at night. In fact, you are going to become more and more aware of the sound of my voice. You're going to focus on the sound of my voice. You will hear and remember everything that I tell you. You will do as I ask, but any other sounds that come into the room will only tend to make you relax more and more, going deeper and deeper, and with each number, you will feel as though you are falling into a deeper and deeper state of relaxation. You are now falling like a leaf, falling from a tree and drifting downward, floating gently to earth, going deeper and deeper as you go down, down, down, relaxing more and more.

Starting with the number 12, in your mind, see it fall off the face of the clock and then just disappear. As you go to sleep, deep, deep asleep:

11, sleep, deep, deep asleep . . .

10, sleep, deep, deep asleep . . .

9, sleep, deep, deep asleep . . .

8, sleep, deep, deep asleep . . .

7, sleep, deep, deep asleep . . .

6, sleep, deep, deep asleep . . .

5, sleep, deep, deep asleep . . .

4, sleep, deep, deep asleep . . .

3, sleep, deep, deep asleep . . .

2, sleep, deep, deep asleep . . .

1, sleep, deep, deep asleep . . .

Feel yourself going deeper and deeper asleep. You continue to see only a white blank face in your mind as you go deep, deep asleep, your body going deeper and deeper asleep, your mind going deep, deep asleep while you concentrate more and more on the sound of my voice . . . the sound of my voice filling the room, filling your head.

You hear and remember everything that I tell you and will do as I ask while your body continues to go deep, deep asleep . . . deep, deep asleep.

Now, in your mind, picture yourself standing at the top of a staircase, and as you look down the staircase, you notice that there are ten steps down. It is a wide, grand staircase. It's got big marble banisters on the sides. The tops of the banisters feel cool to your touch, so hard and cool and smooth as you run your hand over them. And as you look down the stairs, the ten stairs down, you see at the bottom your perfect safe place.

This is a place we are going to create in your mind, a place where you can go to anytime you want. This can be a place from your past—your childhood, perhaps—or it can be someplace you presently like to go to, or a place you would like to go to sometime in the future.

It can be a place that is real, or it can be a place that is totally imagined . . . it's entirely up to you. Any place you would like to go to be alone, to feel safe, to be relaxed—this is a place we are going to build, this is your safe place. But first we have to go down the stairs, one step at a time, and as we take each step down, you will feel ten times more relaxed than you did on the previous step, allowing yourself to go deeper and deeper.

Starting at the top stair, from number 10 step down to . . .

9, and feel yourself relaxing even more . . .

8, going deeper and deeper . . .

7, feeling more and more relaxed . . .

6, going deeper and deeper still . . .

5, it's as though there's a cushion of air under your feet; you can't feel the stairs as you're stepping down; you're becoming lighter and lighter, almost as though you are floating on air . . .

4, going deeper and deeper . . .

3, you are becoming more and more relaxed . . .

2, you can no longer feel the stairs at all below your feet; it's as though you're floating, as you step down to . . .

1, and now from 1 you simply float off the stairs; it's as though you are suspended in the air, completely and totally relaxed, completely and totally relaxed . . .

And now, as you begin to look at your safe spot, you notice first all the objects that are there. I want you to see each and every object clearly in your mind, and the first thing that I want you to think about is the shape of the objects. Look at the shape of each and every object, and as you look at the shapes, begin to see the colors of the objects. Some shapes are square, some are round, some may be triangular.

And now you see the colors, and then, as you begin to look at the objects closer and closer, you can see the patterns and the texture that they are made up from. As you look at them closer, you can see that some of the objects appear to be smooth and hard; some may be rough, others soft and velvety. Whatever they are in your safe place, see each and every object. See the shape, the color, and the textures.

And now, as you continue to look at all the objects in your safe place, begin to notice any smells or aromas that may be there. Any smells—if there is new leather, smell it; if there is a fire burning somewhere, smell it; if there is fresh-cut hay, or grass or flowers, whatever smells might be in your safe place, smell them now.

Any sounds that are in your safe place—I want you now to hear them. Whether it's wind in the trees, or the grass, or water running or lapping at the shore, or fire crackling away—whatever sounds might be in your safe place, hear them. Sounds from the distance, sounds of bells off some-where in the distance, or children laughing and playing—whatever sounds that you would hear, hear them now.

Finally, I want you to just feel what it's like to be here. Feel the peace, the safety, the joy, and the relaxation.

Let it feel like a big, thick wool blanket has descended down over you and you've been tucked in tightly around the edges, perhaps like it did when you were a child. You feel so snug, so secure, so safe. Feel all these things, experience them now: you can see it, you can hear it, you can smell them, you can feel your safe place. Relax and be there, just be there, experiencing your safe place.

Continue to relax. Now, as you relax, I want you to begin looking inward. Turn your eyes and look right inside yourself. Look right down through your rib cage; look right to the center of your being, right to the core of your body. And as you look there, see inside a light suspended, a white light like a mini sun, a ball of energy . . . a white light suspended right in your very core. And as you look at it, you see the white light spreading out, touching all your bones and your muscles, shining through your arms and your legs, lighting up your very center of your body, and you know that this is your core energy. This is your core power. This is all the power and energy any of us have, and it is right inside you, and you can feel it . . . you can feel it. And now you can see it, and you felt it in the past when you've done something that you've been particularly proud of. When you've overcome a big obstacle, when you've met a big challenge, reached a large goal, you've felt that inner warmth and feeling of your ball of energy as it grew bigger and stronger, bigger and stronger.

In the future, anytime you are feeling a little anxious, a little stressed, a little frustrated—anytime you're facing a large challenge, anytime you're overwhelmed by a big goal, anytime you just want to get away, just escape, be by yourself, collect your thoughts, control your mind—anytime at all when you just want to be by yourself, you can come here, come here to your safe place, and all you have to do is this:

Take a deep breath in. As you do, close your eyes and say to your mind, *I'm going to my safe place now*. And then just feel what you feel now; see what you see now; smell and hear what you smell and hear now. Just be here, instantly be here. Just instantly come back to where you are now, and when you get here, you will see that you have all the power and energy inside to face whatever it is you are facing, to meet any challenges that's put before you. You're never given a challenge that you don't have the ability to conquer, and you have the power and the energy to do that, and it's here.

Anytime at all you need to come here to take control of your thoughts and your mind, you can do that. All that you have to do is take a deep breath in . . . relax and be here, even if it is only for a moment. If it's for only a split second, you will find that you can regain control of your emotions and your mind by just closing your eyes and taking a deep breath and saying that *I'm going to my safe place* and seeing and hearing and being where you are now. And when you open your eyes again and return to the present, even if it was only for a second, you will do so feeling so much more powerful, so much more in control, so much more relaxed that you can face any challenge that's put before you. You have the power and the energy; you have all the power and the energy. Now relax and let yourself go even deeper and deeper, becoming more and more relaxed . . .

Imagine you are in the future, walking up to your perfect home, a home you would love to own and live in. This is sometime in the near future, and as you walk up, you feel your hand reach up and touch the front door handle. You feel the cool smoothness of it; you feel the tug of the door as you pull it open and walk in; you feel the comfort and the warmth that surrounds you as you look around the entry, and from the entry, you look down the hall toward your study.

And as you begin to walk down the hallway toward it, with each step you feel yourself going deeper and deeper.

Only 10 steps to go . . .

9, becoming more and more relaxed . . .

8, feeling so comfortable to be home, going toward your study . . .

7, feeling relaxed, very, very relaxed . . .

6, going deeper and deeper . . .

5, closer and closer . . .

4, becoming more and more relaxed . . .

3, going deeper and deeper still . . .

2, feeling so rested, so deep . . .

1, as you stand in the doorway to your study, you are so relaxed, so calm, so comfortable.

From the doorway, you look around the room. You see a large, comfortable chair behind the desk, and you walk around the desk and sit down and sink deeply into the chair. You feel the arms, feel the fabric, smell the aroma of the room.

You hear all the sounds as you look at your desk, the phone, and all the personal items that you would have there.

Then you look at the walls, the pictures, the plaques, the memorabilia that you've collected.

You look back at your desk. Your desk is unique. The drawers on the left have files of all the goals conceived, all arranged alphabetically. Whenever you've thought about a specific goal, all you need to do is go to the file so marked, and all the information you will need will immediately come to your mind.

Know this is true. Ask and you shall receive. Seek and you shall find. Knock and the door shall be open to you. They are all there, all your goals.

On the right side of your desk, the drawers contain all the known people, places, and things of this world, from the very beginning of time. Again, they are all filed so that you can immediately find what you need to confirm your decision to proceed with your goals.

All the great minds are there, waiting for you to ask them to help you. Everyone—Plato, Moses, Saint Thomas Aquinas, Buddha, Jesus of Nazareth, Einstein, Madam Curie, Jim Thorpe, your grandparents, teachers—whomever you need, living or otherwise, from this planet is there. You can access them.

All of your thoughts and energy can be tapped at any time that you choose. Just relax your body and mind and ask for the needed information.

Think of any goal you wish—any goal you wish to achieve—and now you see yourself achieving it. Imagine the goal has already been achieved, and see yourself successful now with the clothes that you would be wearing. See the colors, the textures. See the environment that surrounds you. Smell the smells, the colors and the sounds, and feel the feelings.

Each goal you think of, engage as many of your senses as possible, and see them in your mind. See the people that are there. Hear what they are saying. See the environment. See how others are dressed. And know that when you need help, all that you have to do is turn to your desk . . . in the files, in the files, everything is stored there for you.

Now, as I count down from 3 to 1, I shall remain silent, and you will experience the achievement of your goal.

Put the one goal in your mind that you want to achieve and think about it, and then, when you hear my voice again, it will not distract you. In fact, you will relax and go deeper and deeper still. In the meantime, visualize as clearly as possible you having achieved your goals. See all of the people around you, see where you're at, feel how it feels, smell the smells, hear the sounds.

Are you ready now? Think of your goal and begin to relax. Relax and go deeper and deeper.

3 . . . 2 . . . 1.

Relax and go deeper, deeper, and deeper. Each time that you listen to this, think of a goal—it can be the same goal or a new goal—and allow your mind, allow your imagination, to show or play out the goal. See it in your mind. Hear it. Smell it. Feel it, how it will feel when you accomplish it.

You're doing fine. Take a deep breath and allow yourself to go down deeper and deeper.

And now, this time, I want to try again, and as I count from 3 to 1, I want you to choose a small goal, something very small, something you would like to achieve within the next twenty-four hours.

I want you to see yourself accomplishing this specific goal: feel the positive emotions, the emotions of winning, the enthusiasm, the joy, the freedom, and the confidence—all the things that accomplishing this goal will bring into your life. See yourself in the clothes you'll be wearing, in the environment that will surround you.

Use the unlimited powers of your imagination to project on the screen in your mind this goal that you are going to accomplish within the next twenty-four hours. See it now clearly as I count down . . .

3 . . .

2, going deeper and deeper . . .

1 . . .

Notice how good it makes you feel. Relax take a deep breath, and still go deeper and deeper . . . deeper and deeper.

Each and every time you listen to this, you'll play the same or new goals, and you'll find that goals begin to become a part of your life. You'll instinctively practice and make new goals each day, and you'll begin to notice how easily they begin to come to you, how quickly you'll accomplish them. They'll become infectious. Each and every day you'll want to set new goals—new goals for the next twenty-four hours and new goals for your lifetime. And each time you listen to this, you'll see them clearly in your mind, and the clearer you see them, the quicker and easier they will come to you.

And now, in a moment, we are going to come back to the room. We're going to come back very, very slowly by my counting 1 to 5.

You will not open your eyes until we get to 5.

1, begin to notice a feeling returning to your arms, legs, hands, or feet. You may notice a tingling sensation: that's perfectly natural. It will soon go away . . .

2, you begin to hear the sounds of the room . . .

3, you feel your eyes have been bathed in a cool mountain stream. They are so alive, so sharp, so focused . . .

4, you just have a general sense of well-being around you. You feel better and better than ever before . . .

And now, before I say 5, I want you to lock firmly in your mind all these goals, the goals that you've set for yourself for over the next twenty-four hours and the goal that you've been concentrating on in this session. Set them firmly in your mind. Say that you accept these suggestions. You will achieve these goals.

5 . . . open your eyes and come back to the room.

To Write to the Author

If you wish to contact the author or would like more information about this book, please write to the author in care of Llewellyn Worldwide and we will forward your request. Both the author and publisher appreciate hearing from you and learning of your enjoyment of this book and how it has helped you. Llewellyn Worldwide cannot guarantee that every letter written to the author can be answered, but all will be forwarded. Please write to:

Layton Park
℅ Llewellyn Worldwide
2143 Wooddale Drive, Dept. 0-7387-1052-0
Woodbury, MN 55125-2989, U.S.A.
Please enclose a self-addressed stamped envelope for reply,
or $1.00 to cover costs. If outside of the U.S.A.,
enclose international postal reply coupon.

Many of Llewellyn's authors have websites with additional information and resources. For more information, please visit our website at:
www.llewellyn.com